Yorkshire Lists of Names

Stuart A. Raymond

Yorkshire: The Genealogists Library Guide 3

Published by the
Federation of Family History Societies (Publications) Ltd.,
Units 15-16 Chesham Industrial Estate
Oram Street, Bury, Lancashire, BL9 6EN, UK.

Copies also obtainable from:
S.A. & M.J. Raymond, P.O.Box 35, Exeter, EX1 3YZ, U.K.

First published 2000

ISBN: 1 86006 120 6 (FFHS (Publications) Ltd)

ISBN: 1 899668 12 8 (S.A. & M.J. Raymond)

ISSN: 1033-2065

Printed and bound by The Alden Group, London and Northampton.

Contents

Front cover: Statue of the Black Prince, Leeds

Introduction

This bibliography is intended primarily for genealogists. It is, however, hoped that it will also prove useful to historians, librarians, archivists, research students, and anyone else interested in the history of Yorkshire. It is intended to be used in conjunction with my *English genealogy: a bibliography,* and the other volumes in the *British genealogical library guides* series. A full list of these volumes currently in print appears on the back cover.

Lists of names are vital sources of information for genealogists, since they provide one means of locating ancestors in time and place. This volume identifies a wide range of lists and indexes of names relating to the historic county of Yorkshire, especially those relating to tax records, voting, and the census. Directories are also included here, as these are primarily lists of names. This volume complements the other volumes of *Yorkshire: the genealogists library guide,* which ought also to be consulted. In general, I have not repeated information here which is contained in other volumes. Volume 1 is devoted to general information on the county's history, bibliography, archives, journals, *etc.,* volume 2 identifies published parish registers, monumental inscriptions, and probate records; works on the administrative records of state, church and estates are listed in volume 4; volume 5 is devoted to occupational sources; pedigrees, family histories, *etc.,* are listed in vol.6. The whole work is exclusively concerned with published works, and thousands of books and journal articles are listed. Numerous microfiche publications are also listed. However, the innumerable notes and queries to be found in family history society journals etc., are excluded, except where their content is of importance. Where I have included such notes, replies to them are cited in the form 'see also', with no reference to the names of respondents. I have also excluded extracts from newspapers, and works which have not been published. Where possible, citations are accompanied by annotations giving further information which might be of use. I have physically examined almost every item listed here, with the exception of some long runs of directories, where every volume may not have been checked. Items which have not been seen are annotated 'not seen', as I have not been able to check the correct title or the contents.

Be warned: just because information has been published, it does not necessarily follow that it is accurate. I have not made any judgement on the accuracy of most works listed: that is up to you.

Anyone who tries to compile a totally comprehensive bibliography of Yorkshire is likely to fall short of his aim. The task is almost impossible, especially if the endeavour is made by one person. That does not, however, mean that the attempt should not be made. This bibliography is as comprehensive as I have been able to make it. However, usefulness, rather than comprehensiveness, has been my prime aim - and this book would not be useful to anyone if its publication were to be prevented by a vain attempt to ensure total comprehensiveness. I am well aware that there are likely to be omissions, especially in view of the fact that, given constraints of time and money, it has not been possible for me to visit all of the large number of libraries with substantial collections on Yorkshire's history. Each of them may well possess works not held anywhere else. The identification of such works is not, however, a major aim of this bibliography. Rather, my purpose has been to enable you to identify works which are mostly readily available. Some titles you may be able to purchase; all can be found in libraries throughout the English-speaking world. You can check the holdings of many libraries via their catalogues on the internet; alternatively, if your local library does not hold a particular book, the librarian should be able to tell you where to find it and, as a last resort, may be able to borrow it for you via the inter-library loan network, irrespective of whether you live in London or San Francisco. The libraries of family history societies are also worth checking - even if they are far distant from Yorkshire: for example, the Genealogical Society of Victoria, in Melbourne, has a good collection of books on English genealogy. Some family history societies offer a postal borrowing service; others may be willing to check a particular book for you. It is also worth joining one of the genealogical newsgroups or mailing lists on the internet; other members may hold the books you need, and be willing to check them for you.

Trade directories may be particularly difficult to track down: they may usually be found in the local studies libraries of the area they cover, and perhaps in the British Library, but otherwise they are rare, and unlikely to be available via interlibrary loan. However, reprints are increasingly becoming available on microfiche, and I have indicated where this is the case.

Consultation of my *British Genealogical Microfiche* will enable you to identify a number of publishers of reprinted directories on fiche.

If you are an assiduous researcher, you may well come across items I have missed. If you do, please let me know, so that they can be included in the next edition.

The work of compiling this bibliography has depended heavily on the resources of the libraries I have used. These included the local studies collections in the public libraries of Bradford, Doncaster, Hull, Leeds, Sheffield, and York, the Brotherton Library at the University of Leeds, the British Library, the Society of Genealogists, Guildhall Library, the University and the Central Library in Bristol, the University of Exeter library and the Exeter Public Library in Exeter. I have also used the resources of a number of family history societies, and am particularly grateful to the societies for Devon, Cornwall, Somerset & Dorset, Sheffield and Ripon/Harrogate. All these institutions deserve my thanks, as does John Perkins, who read and commented on an early draft of the book. Mary Raymond typed the manuscript, Mark Gant undertook the task of indexing, and Bob Boyd saw the book through the press. I am grateful too to the officers of the Federation of Family History Societies, whose support is vital for the continuation of this series. My thanks also to my wife Marjorie.

Stuart A. Raymond

Abbreviations

B.A.	*Bradford Antiquary*
B.S.H.S.	*Bulletin of the Saddleworth Historical Society.*
B.T.	*Banyan tree: journal of the East Yorkshire Family History Society*
C.T.L.H.S.B.	*Cleveland and Teeside Local History Society*
C.Y.D.F.H.S.J.	*City of York & District Family History Society journal*
C.Y.D.F.H.S.N.	*City of York & District Family History Society newsletter*
Cameo	*Cameo: Morley & District Family History Group newsletter*
Don. Anc.	*Doncaster Ancestor*
E.Y.F.H.S.	East Yorkshire Family History Society
E.Y.F.H.S., M.I.	East Yorkshire Family History Society monumental inscriptions
F.H.S.	Family History Society
F.S.	*Flowing stream: journal of Sheffield and District Family History Society*
H. & D.F.H.S.	Huddersfield & District Family History Society
H. & D.F.H.S.J.	*Huddersfield & District Family History Society journal*
J.Cl.F.H.S.	*Journal of the Cleveland Family History Society*
K.D.F.H.S.J.	*Keighley & District Family History Society journal*
N.Y.C.R.O.P.	North Yorkshire County Record Office Publications
O.W.R.	*Old West Riding*
P.R.H.A.S.	*Papers, reports, etc., read before the Halifax Antiquarian Society.*
R.H.	*Ripon historian*
T.E.R.A.S.	*Transactions of the East Riding Archaeological Society*
T. Hal.A.S.	*Transactions of the Halifax Archaeological Society*
T. Hunter A.S.	*Transactions of the Hunter Archaeological Society*
T.S.	Thoresby Society
Wh.N.	*Wharfedale newsletter: the journal of the Wharfedale Family History Group*
Y.A.J.	*Yorkshire archaeological journal*

Y.A.S., F.H.P.S.S.	Yorkshire Archaeological Society. Family History and Population Studies Section
Y.A.S., F.H.P.S.S.N.	*Yorkshire Archaeological Society. Family History and Population Studies Section Newsletter*
Y.A.S., R.S.	Yorkshire Archaeological Society. Record Series
Y.C.M.	*Yorkshire county magazine*
Y.F.H.	*Yorkshire family historian*
Y.F.H.S.N.	*York Family History Society Newsletter*
Y.G.	*Yorkshire genealogist*
Y.N.Q.I.	*Yorkshire notes & queries* [1888-90]
Y.N.Q.II.	*Yorkshire notes & queries* [1905-9]

Bibliographic Presentation

Authors names are in SMALL CAPITALS. Book and journal titles are in *italics*. Articles appearing in journals, and chapters of books *etc*. are in inverted commas and textface type. Volume numbers are in **bold** and the individual number of the journal may be shown in parentheses. These are normally followed by the place of publication (except where this is London, which is omitted), the name of the publisher and the date of publication. In the case of articles, further figures indicate page numbers.

Libraries and Record Offices

Many libraries have substantial collections of books and journals on Yorkshire history, and the addresses given below are only amongst the most important. I have not included the addresses of most family history societies, most of which have libraries available to members, which ought to be used by everyone tracing their ancestors in the area covered. These addresses change frequently, and any listing would be out of date by the time it was printed. Current addresses are regularly published in *Family history news & digest.*

I have also not included the addresses of most Yorkshire record repositories. These hold the archives you may need to consult, but generally speaking do not have large collections of printed books.

It is also worth pointing out that many public and university libraries throughout the English-speaking world hold much Yorkshire material; in particular, many university libraries subscribe to major series such as the *Yorkshire archaeological journal* and the Yorkshire Archaeological Society's *Record series* — which may also be available in the libraries of other county historical societies, many of which exchange journals with each other.

Major collections of Yorkshire material are to be found in at least two London institutions:

> British Library
> 96, Euston Road,
> London,
> NW1 2DB

> Society of Genealogists,
> 14, Charterhouse Buildings,
> Goswell Road,
> London,
> EC1M 7BA

The two Yorkshire institutions with a county-wide remit are:

> Borthwick Institute,
> University of York,
> St.Anthony's Hall
> Peasholme Green,
> York,
> YO1 2PW

> Yorkshire Archaeological Society
> Claremont,
> 23, Clarendon Road,
> Leeds,
> LS2 9NZ

A number of university libraries in the county have important Yorkshire collections:

> Brynmor Jones Library,
> University of Hull,
> Hull, HU6 7RX
> (Houses the East Yorkshire Bibliography)

> Brotherton Library
> University of Leeds
> Leeds, LS2 9JT

The major local collections in public libraries are:

> **Bradford**
> Bradford Central Library
> Princes Way,
> Bradford,
> BD1 1NN

> **Hull**
> Local Studies Library,
> Hull Central Library
> Albion Street,
> Hull, HU1 3TF

Leeds
Local History Collection,
Central Library,
Calverley Street,
Leeds, LS1 3AB

Middlesbrough
Local Collection,
Middlesbrough Reference Library,
Victoria Square,
Middlesbrough,
Cleveland,
TS1 2AY

Sheffield
Local Studies Library,
Sheffield City Libraries,
Surrey Street,
Sheffield, S1 1XZ

York
York City Library,
Reference Library,
Local Studies Collection,
Museum Street,
York, YO1 2DS

1. TAX RECORDS

The records of government taxation are voluminous, and provide us with innumerable lists of taxpayers. Many — but by no means all — of the lists relating to Yorkshire have been published, and are listed below. For the genealogist, these lists provide invaluable means of locating ancestors in time and place.

A. *Subsidies and Poll Taxes*

Subsidies were one of the major sources of governmental revenue prior to the 17th century; the tax exacted from everyone capable of paying. Poll taxes were also of some importance — although governments did take note of the Peasants Revolt, caused by the poll tax of 1381. Taxation was an inexact science, and the limitations and unreliability of early 16th century subsidy returns for Yorkshire and Lancashire are discussed in:

HOYLE, R.W. 'Resistance and manipulation in early Tudor taxation: some evidence from the North', *Archives* **20**(90), 1993, 158-76.

A number of returns for the whole county have been published:

1297

BROWN, WILLIAM, ed. *Yorkshire lay subsidy, being a ninth collected in 25 Edward I (1297)*. Y.A.S., R.S. **16**. 1894.

1301

BROWN, WILLIAM, ed. *Yorkshire lay subsidy, being a fifteenth collected 30 Edward I (1301)*. Y.A.S., R.S. **21**. 1897.

1327-8

PARKER, J.W.R., ed. 'Lay subsidy rolls, I Edward III', in *Miscellanea* **2**. Y.A.S., R.S. **74**. 1929, 104-71.

Agbrigg & Morley Wapentakes

CARTWRIGHT, JAMES J. 'A subsidy roll for the Wapentakes of Agbrigg and Morley of the 15th Henry VIII', *Y.A.J.* **2**, 1873, 43-60. 1523-4.

'Lay subsidies of York, West Riding, 207/186: Wapentakes of Aggbrigg and Morley *anno* 1545', in *Miscellanea* **[3]**. *T.S.* 1899, 311-16; *Miscellanea* **[4]**. *T.S.* **11**, 1904, 101-29 & 333-68.

BRIGG, WILLIAM, ed. 'Lay subsidy 262/4, Wapentake of Agbrigg and Morley, *anno* 1588', in *Miscellanea* **[5]**. *T.S.* **15**, 1909, 132-51.

Barkston Ash & Agbrigg Wapentakes

'Rotuli collectorum subsidii regi a laicis anno secundo concessi in Westrythyngo in Comitatu Eboraci', *Y.A.J.* **6**, 1881, 129-71. Poll tax, 1378-9, Wapentakes of Barkston Ash and Agbrigg.

Bradford

'The poll tax in Bradford', *Y.N.Q.II.* **2**, 1906, 329. Transcript of the return for 1378 (including Manningham).

Calverley cum Farsley, *etc.*

'Lay subsidies, W.R. No. 210/394a, hearth tax, Lady Day 1666', *Y.C.M.* **3**, 1893, 53-5. For Calverley cum Farsley, and Tong.

Claro Wapentake

'Rotuli collectorum subsidii regi a laicis anno scundo concessi in Westrythyngo in Comitatu Eboracci', *Y.A.J.* **7**, 1882, 6-31. Poll Tax, 1378-9, Claro Wapentake.

Cowling

'Lay subsidy, Yorkshire 206/116, 14 & 15 Henry VIII ... Collyng', *B.A.* N.S. **3**, 1912, 121. i.e. Cowling.

Craven

HOYLE, R.W., ed. *Early Tudor Craven: subsidies and assessments, 1510-1547.* Y.A.S., R.S. **145**. 1987.

East Riding

LLOYD, ELEANOR. 'Poll tax returns for the East Riding, 4 Ric. II', *Y.A.J.* **20**, 1908-9, 318-52. 1380-1.

COX, J. CHARLES. 'A poll-tax of the East Riding, with some account of the Peasant Revolt of 1381', *T.E.R.A.S.* **15**, 1909, 1-70. See also **27**, 1934, 81-97. Tax of 1378-9. The Howdenshire portion is also available separately; see below.

LLOYD, ELEANOR. 'East Yorkshire subsidy rolls, 2 Charles I', *T.E.R.A.S.* **14**, 1907, 67-73. For 1626-7.

Giggleswick

BRAYSHAW, THOS. *Parish of Giggleswick: poll tax, A.D. 1379; followers of Lord Clifford, A.D. 1510; Association for the Prosecution of Felons, A.D. 1743; Land tax &c., A.D. 1800.* Stackhouse: Thos. Brayshaw, 1884.

Grassington

CRAGG. R.B. 'Grassington: a poll tax 1698', *Y.N.Q.II.* **1**, 1905, 210. List of taxpayers.

Halifax

LISTER, J., OGDEN, J.H., eds. *Poll tax (lay subsidy) 2 Richard II (1379): parish of Halifax, in the Wapontake of Morley ... with notes on local returns; also rental of Halifax and Heptonstall, 1439.* Halifax Antiquarian Society record series **1**. 1906. Reprinted from *Y.A.J.* **6**. Includes copious 'notes of identification.'

Howdenshire

'Assessment roll of the poll-tax for Howdenshire, *etc.,* in the second year of the reign of King Richard II (1379)', *Y.A.J.* **9**, 1886, 129-62.

SALTMARSHE, PHILIP. 'Local history from the Howdenshire poll tax roll', *T.E.R.A.S.* **27**, 1934, 81-97. Discussion of the roll for 1379.

Hull

CAWLEY, A., ed. *The people of Hull in 1695 and 1697: an index to the poll tax assessments.* Hull: Kingston upon Hull City Council / East Yorkshire Family History Society, 1987.

Keighley

'Lay subsidy Yorkshire 206/116 (14 and 15 Hen. VIII) ... villa de Kyghtley', *B.A.* N.S., **3**, 1912, 114. i.e. Keighley.

Kirkby Overblow

CONNELL, E.J. 'The Kirkby Overblow poll tax of 1379', *Yorkshire history quarterly* **2**(2), 1996, 85-6. Brief discussion.

Leeds

RUSBY, JAMES. 'Leeds borough subsidy', in *Miscellanea* **1**. *T.S.* **2**. 1891, 22-5. For 1596-7.

Morley

BLAIR, AUDREY. 'Poll tax', *Cameo* 1990, no. 1, unpaginated. Morley poll tax, 1379.

'1379 poll tax for Morley', *Cameo* 1993, no. 2, 14-16. Lists taxpayers.

Morley, Skyrack & Claro Wapentakes

'Rotuli collectorum subsidii regi a laicis anno secundo concessi in Westrythyngo in Comitatu Ebor', *Y.A.J.* **6**, 1881, 287-312. Poll tax, 1378-9, for the Wapentakes of Morley, Skyrack and Claro.

Osgoldcross Wapentake

'Rotuli collectorum subsidii regi a laicis in Westythyngo in comitatu Ebor', *Y.A.J.* **6**, 1881, 1-44. Poll tax, 1378-9, Osgoldcross Wapentake.

Skyrack Wapentake

CARTWRIGHT, JAMES J. 'A subsidy roll for the Wapentake of Skyrack of the 15th Henry VIII', *Y.A.J.* **2**, 1873, 289-96. 1523-4.

'Lay subsidy 207/200, Wapentake of Skyrack 30 June and 20 October 1545', in *Miscellanea* **[3]**. *T.S.* **9**, 1899, 126-52.

'Lay subsidy, 207/194: Wapentake of Skyrack, 12 Feb., 37 Henry VIII, 1545-6', in *Miscellanea* **[3]**. *T.S.* **9**, 1899, 153-60.

'Lay subsidy, 208/285, Wapentake of Skyrack, *anno* 1588', in *Miscellanea* **[5]**. *T.S.* **15**, 1909, 38-45.

'Subsidy roll of the Wapentake of Skyrack, 1610', in *Miscellanea* **[6]**. *T.S.* **22**. 1915, 108-17.

STANSFELD, JOHN. 'Subsidy roll of the Wapentake of Skyrack, in the West Riding of Yorkshire, 1621', in *Miscellanea*. **1**. *T.S.* **2**, 1891, 62-97.

Staincliffe & Ewcross Wapentakes, *etc.*

'Rotuli collectorum subsidii regi a laicis anno secundo concessi in Westrythngo in Comitatu Eboraci', *Y.A.J.* **7**, 1882, 145-86. Poll tax, 1378/9, Wapentakes of Staincliffe, Ewcross and the Ainsty.

Staincross Wapentake
'Rotuli collectorum subsidi regi a laicis anno secundo concessi in Westrythyngo Comitatu Eboraci', *Y.A.J.* **5**, 1879, 417-432. Poll tax, 1378-9, Staincross Wapentake.
'Subsidy roll of the Wapentake of Staincross, in the West Riding of Yorkshire, in 1663', *Collectanea genealogica et topographica* **3**, 1836, 333-8.

Strafford Wapentake
'Rotuli collectorum subsidii regi a laicis anno secundo concessi in Westrythyngo in comitatu Eboraci', *Y.A.J.* **5**, 1879, 1-51. Poll-tax, Strafford Wapentake, 1378-9.

Tickhill Wapentake
'Rotuli collectorum subsidii regi a laicis anno secundo concessi in Westrythygno in comitatu Eboraci', **5**, 1879, 241-66. Poll tax, Tickhill Wapentake, 1378-9.

West Riding
CLARK, GEO. T. 'The West Riding poll-tax and lay subsidy rolls, 2d Richard II', *Y.A.J.* **7**, 1882, 187-93. For 1378-9.

York
STELL, P.M., & $HAWKYARD, ALASDAIR. 'The lay subsidy of 1334 for York', *York historian* **13**, 1996, 2-14. Transcript.
LEGGETT, JENNIFER I., ed. 'The 1377 poll tax for the City of York', *Y.A.J.* **43**, 1971, 128-46.
BARTLETT, NEVILLE, ed. 'The lay poll tax returns for the City of York in 1381', *T.E.R.A.S.* **30**, 1953, 1-90.
'Subsidy roll for York and Ainsty', *Y.A.J.* **4**, 1877, 170-201. For 1524.

B. *The Hearth Tax*.
The hearth tax was granted to replace the subsidy following the return of Charles II from exile in 1660. An extensive study of the Yorkshire returns, with detailed lists of them (but no names) is provided by:

PURDY, J.D. *Yorkshire hearth tax returns*. University of Hull studies in regional and local history **7**. Hull: University of Hull Centre for Regional and Local History, 1991.

Agbrigg & Morley Wapentakes
The hearth tax list for Agbrigg and Morley Wapentakes, West Riding of Yorkshire, Lady Day 1672. 2 vols. Ripon: Ripon Historical Society/ Ripon, Harrogate & District Family History Group, 1992. v. 1. Township lists. v. 2. Surname index.

Ardsley
HARRISON, D., & RITCHIE, J. 'Ardsley hearth tax 1672', *Barnsley F.H.S. newsletter* October 1992, 12.

Barkston Ash & Osgoldcross Wapentakes
The hearth tax list for Barkston Ash and Osgoldcross Wapentakes, West Riding of Yorkshire, Lady Day 1672. Ripon: Ripon Historical Society / Ripon Harrogate & District Family History Group, 1994.

Brandesburton, *etc.*
'Hearth tax returns', *B.T.* **23**, 1985, 19. For Brandesburton, Barmston, and Bonick and Dunnington. Undated (but late 17th c.)

Claro Wapentake
The hearth tax list for Claro Wapentake, West Riding of Yorkshire, Lady Day 1672. Ripon: Ripon Historical Society / Ripon, Harrogate & District Family History Group, 1990.

Dickering and Holderness Wapentakes
The hearth tax list for Dickering, North, Mid and South Holdernesse Wapentakes, East Riding of Yorkshire, Lady Day 1672. Ripon: Ripon Historical Society / Ripon, Harrogate & District Family History Group, 1996.

Halifax
CLEGG, C. 'Hearth and window taxes', *P.R.H.A.S.* 1913, 275302. Includes Halifax hearth tax, 1666, *etc.*

Howden Wapentake, *etc.*
The hearth tax list for Howden, Ouze and Darwent, Harthill Holme Beacon, Harthill Wilton, and Buckrose Wapentakes, East Riding of Yorkshire, Lady Day, 1672. Ripon: Ripon Historical Society / Ripon, Harrogate & District Family History Group, 1996.

Hull, *etc.*

The hearth tax list for the town and county of Hull, and Harthill Hunsley and Harthill Bainton Beacon Wapentakes, East Riding of Yorkshire, Lady Day 1672. Ripon: Ripon Historical Society / Ripon Harrogate & District Family History Group, 1996.

Lund

'Lund', *B.T.* **26**, 1986, 22-4. Includes hearth tax, 1673-4, list of landowners at enclosure, 1794, *etc.*

Kirby Wiske

'Hearth tax, temp Charles II, undated. Parish of Kirby Wiske', *J.Cl.F.H.S.* **5**(1), 1992, 35-8. Transcript.

North Riding

The hearth tax list for the North Riding of Yorkshire, Michaelmas 1673. 5 pts. Ripon: Ripon Historical Society / Ripon, Harrogate & District Family History Group, 1991. Pt. 1. Gilling West and Hang West Wapentakes. Pt. 2. Allerton, Gilling East, Halikeld, and Hang East Wapentakes. Pt. 3. Birdforth and Bulmer Wapentakes. Pt. 4. Rydale, Pickering Lith, & Scarborough Wapentakes. Pt 5. Langbarugh West, Langbarugh East and Whitby Strand Wapentakes.

Osgoldcross Wapentake

SYKES, DR. 'Exchequer lay subsidy rolls. Bundle 210, no. 393. Hearth tax roll, no. 16, Charles II [1666]. The Wapentake of Osgoldcross', *Y.G.* **2**, 1890, 196-216.

Redcar

'Public Record Office, Chancery Lane, London. E179/261/35. Hearth tax assessment roll, Charles II: Langbaurgh Wapentake, Redcar', *J.Cl.F.H.S.* **2**(6), 1984, 12.

Richmond

FIELDHOUSE, R.T. 'The hearth tax and social structure in the borough of Richmond in 1673', *C.T.L.H.S.B.* **14**, 1971, 9-17. See also **15**, 1971-2, 15. Not a transcript, but mentions some names.

Saddleworth

BRIERLEY, MORGAN. 'The hearth tax in Saddleworth, 1668', *Palatine note-book* **3**, 1883, 216-7. Transcript.

Sheffield

'Hearth tax returns for Sheffield, Lady Day, 1672', *F.S.* **2**(3), 1980, 65; **2**(4), 1980, 101-2; **3**(1), 1981, 24-5; **3**(2), 1981, 46-7.

Silkstone

HARRISON, D., & RITCHIE, J., eds. *Hearth tax return 1672: parish of Silkstone.* [Barnsley]: Barnsley F.H.S., [1997].

Skelton, *etc.*

'Hearth tax rolls ... Langbaurgh, E179/261/35', *J.Cl.F.H.S.* **2** (9), 1985, 20-22. For Skelton, Kirkleatham, Upleatham and Marske; date not given (but late 17th c.)

Skyrack Wapentake

STANSFELD, JOHN. 'Return of the hearth tax for the Wapentake of Skyrack, A.D. 1672', in *Miscellanea* **1**. *T.S.* **2**, 1891, 180-204; *Miscellanea* **2**. *T.S.* **4**. 1895, 17-36.

South Yorkshire

HEY, DAVID, ed. *The hearth tax returns for South Yorkshire, Ladyday, 1672.* Sheffield: University of Sheffield Division of Continuing Education, 1991. Covers Wapentakes of Strafford & Tickhill, and Staincross.

Staincliffe & Ewcross Wapentakes

The hearth tax list for Staincliffe and Ewcross Wapentakes, West Riding of Yorkshire, Lady Day 1672. Ripon: Ripon Historical Society / Ripon Harrogate & District Family History Group, 1992.

Wakefield

The hearth tax returns of 1672 for the Wakefield Metropolitan District, and a Wakefield census of 1723. Published as *Wakefield Historical Society Journal* **5**, 1978.

York and the Ainsty
The hearth tax list for York city parishes and Ainsty Wapentake, Lady Day, 1672. Ripon: Ripon Historical Society / Ripon, Harrogate & District Family History Group, 1992.

C. *The Land Tax*
Returns made for the land tax are an important source for the 18th and 19th centuries, although relatively few returns have been published. For a brief description, based on West Riding records, see:
UNWIN, R.W. *Search guide to the English land tax.* Wakefield: West Yorkshire County Record Office, 1982.
See also:
NOBLE, MARGARET. 'Land tax returns and urban development', *Local historian* 15(2), 1982, 86-92. Methodological discussion, using returns of six East Riding towns, 1780-1830.

Barnsley
UNWIN, ROBERT. 'An industrial dimension to land tax studies: The Barnsley coalfield, 1690-1830', in TURNER, MICHAEL, & MILLS, DENNIS, eds. *Land and property: the English land tax 1692-1832.* Gloucester: Alan Sutton, 1986, 136-57. Includes various assessments.

Bradford
EMPSALL, T.T. 'Land and property tax 1704', *B.A.* **1**, 1888, 53-4, 110-11 & 167-70; **2**, 1895, 15-18. Transcript for Bradford, *etc.*
'An assessment for raising the sum of one hundred and ninety nine pounds five shillings and two pence charged upon the town of Bradford for His Majesty's use for the present year 1727', *B.A.* N.S. **2**, 1905, 135-41. Land tax.

Brandesburton
'Land tax assessment 1782', *B.T.* **12**, 1982, 9. For Bradesburton.

Flamborough
'[Flamborough]', *B.T.* **15**, 1983, 12-14. Includes land tax assessment, 1783, 1851 census, and extracts from Baines *directory* for 1823.

Giggleswick
See above under Subsidies

Kilham
'Kilham land tax 1730', *B.T.* **19**, 1984, 23.

Morley
'Touching the rates and values of lands, and the ways of assessing, in Morley Division, in 1699', *Y.C.M.* **4**, 1894, 109-16. Presumably for the land tax.
'West Riding of the County of York: Morley Division, 1693', *B.A.* **1**, 1888, 235. Lists collectors for an aid of 1693; by township.
FEDERER, CHARLES A., ed. 'West Riding of the County of York, Morley Division: assessment, on land in the year 1692-3', *B.A.* N.S. **1**, 1900, 122-33.

Sowerby
DENT. G. 'The taxpayers of Sowerby 1750-1758', *T.Hal.A.S.* 1936, 235-46. Includes land tax assessment 1750 and 1753, also poor rate 1758.

D. *Other Taxes*
A variety of other tax imposts have left traces in British archives. For an early survey of the taxable capacity of the country, see:

[SCAIFE, R.H.], ed. *The survey of the County of York, taken by John de Kirkby, commonly called Kirkby's inquest; also inquisitions of Knights fees, the nomina villarum for Yorkshire, and an appendix of illustrative documents.* Surtees Society **49**. 1867. Lists Knights fees in the reign of Edward I (1272-1307); also includes return for part of the West Riding of an 'aid' collected in 1302, grants relating to wardships and marriages, 12-13th c., *etc.*

Feudal aids levied in Sheffield are listed in:
ADDY, S.O. 'A book of feudal aids made for the Earl of Shrewsbury in 1451', *T. Hunter A.S.* **1**(2), 1916, 137-72.

A number of brief notes relate to miscellaneous taxes post-1695:
CARTWRIGHT, J.J. 'List of persons in Yorkshire who paid the tax on male servants in 1780', *Y.A.J.* **14**, 1896-7, 65-80.

JACKSON, MOREEN. 'From Heptonstall parish registers: list of batchelors & widdowers to pay tax 1696', *Y.F.H.* **14**(5), 1988, 123.

GOODCHILD, JOHN. 'Taxation in the Wakefield area in the eighteenth and nineteenth centuries: a preliminary note on the Division of Lower Agbrigg', *Newsletter / Y.A.S. Local History Study Section* **26**, 1985, 7-11; 27, 1986, 3-5. Discussion of a range of miscellaneous taxes, e.g. the horse tax, 1785, hairpowder tax, etc.

THOMPSON, H.W. 'The tax on bachelors and widowers imposed in 1695', in *Miscellanea* [7]. *T.S.* **24**, 1919, 362-67. For Skyrack Wapentake; names of collectors only.

2. OATHS OF ALLEGIENCE: THE PROTESTATION, *etc.*

Political unrest in England has on occasion persuaded governments to secure support by taking an oath of allegiance. The commencement of civil war was one such occasion; the protestation oath was demanded from all adult males. The survival rate for Yorkshire returns has not been good, and only a few returns have been published. See:

Agbrigg Wapentake
LINDLEY, R.P. 'The 1642 census', *H. & D.F.H.S.* **6**(3), 1993, 82-3. List of protestation returns for Agbrigg Wapentake, with transcript for Hepworth.

Bradford
'Protestation returns 1641', *B.A.* **12**; N.S., **10**(47), 1982, 138-45. Transcript for Bradford.

Halifax
CLAY, CHARLES T. 'The Protestation of 1641: a harbinger of the Covenant', *P.R.H.A.S.* 1919, 105-15.

Sessay cum Heaton
'The protestation returns 1641/2', *Y.F.H.S.N.* **14**, 1986, 21-3. Brief note, with facsimile for Sessay cum Heaton.

The oath of allegiance taken in 1723 in York also lists many signatures; it is transcribed in:

JONES, BRIAN. *York oath of allegiance 1723.* Bradford: Brian Jones, 1998.

3. POLL BOOKS AND ELECTORAL REGISTERS

Poll books record the names of those who voted in Parliamentary elections; electoral registers list those entitled to vote. Many were published, but copies of the originals are now scarce; full lists are given in two of the *Gibson guides* (see my *English Genealogy* for details). A number of volumes have been reprinted in recent years and are listed here.

The Yorkshire poll book 1741. Facsimile reprint. Exeter: S.A. & M.J. Raymond, 1997.
The Yorkshire poll book, 1807. Facsimile reprint. Exeter: S.A. & M.J. Raymond, *Forthcoming.*
The Yorkshire West Riding poll book 1835. Exeter: S.A. & M.J. Raymond, [1996].

Allerton
PERKINS, JOHN P. '1807 poll book for Allerton, North Yorkshire', *J.Cl.F.H.S.* 6(2), 1995, 25-8.

Beverley
The poll for the town of Beverley, 9th June 1826. 1 fiche. Society of Genealogists, 1996.
The poll for the borough of Beverley, 30th June 1841. 1 fiche. Society of Genealogists, 1996.
Electoral register, Borough of Beverley, 30th November 1862- 1st December 1863. 2 fiche. Society of Genealogists, 1996.

Bilton, *etc.*
'The poll for the County of York 1807', *R.H.* 2(9), 1995, 226-9. Extracts for Bilton with Harrogate, Knaresborough, Pannal, and Scriven.

Giggleswick
BRAYSHAW, THOS. *Parliamentary electors of the parish of Giggleswick, A.D. 1708-1849.* Stackhouse: Thos. Brayshaw, 1886.

Hull
BARNARD, ROBERT. *Hull poll books as directories.* Hull: Hull College Local History Unit, 1997. Indexes the Hull poll books for 1747, 1774 and 1780, and the Hull portion of the Yorkshire pollbook 1741.
The Hull poll book 1835. Exeter: S.A. & M.J. Raymond, 1997.

Knaresborough
ATKINSON, W.A. 'A Parliamentary election in Knaresborough in 1628', *Y.A.J.* **34,** 1939, 213-21.

Leeds
MORRIS, R.J. 'Property titles and the use of British urban poll books for social analysis *Urban history yearbook* 1983, 29-38. Methodological essay, based on the Leeds poll book 1832.

Wakefield & District
The register of persons entitled to vote at any election of a member or members to serve in Parliament in the Southern Division of the West Riding of the County of York between the 30th of November 1861 and the 1st December 1862, within the Wakefield polling district. Wakefield: Charles Heneage Elsley, 1861. Facsimile reprint, Pontefract: Pontefract & District F.H.S., 1998.

York
JONES, BRIAN, ed. *The poll for members in Parliament to represent the City of York, 1774.* Bradford: Brian Jones, 1999.
HAYWOOD, KEN. 'York World War One index', *C.Y.D.F.H.S.N.* **18,** 1988, 24-7. Description of an index to absent voters (mostly servicemen), and to the *Kings book of York fallen heroes.*

4. THE CENSUS

Much the most useful lists, from the genealogists point of view, are those deriving from nineteenth century censuses. Innumerable indexes, *etc.,* are available for Yorkshire; they are listed here by date and place. For registration districts, see:

NAYLOR, TONY. 'The population of Bradford', *Bod-Kin* **41**, 1995, 15-21. Lists districts and sub-districts used in the censuses, 1841-91.

NAYLOR, TONY. 'The census registration districts surrounding Bradford', *Bod-Kin* **2**(6), 1998, 16-18.

Population Listings, etc.

Apart from the official census, many other population listings have been compiled. For full details, see the works listed in my *English genealogy.* A number of Yorkshire listings are in print:

Bradford

JONES, BRIAN. *Bradford population listings.* 2 vols. Bradford: Brian Jones, 1995. Lists from various sources e.g. land tax 1712, valuation book 1839, list of constables, *etc.*

JONES, BRIAN. *Population listings for the area of Westgate, Bradford 1780, and Bradford and part of Little Horton, 1804.* Bradford: B. Jones, 1995.

Wakefield

JONES, BRIAN. *An account of the numbers of families, communicants and souls in Wakefield town and parish 1723.* Bradford: Brian Jones, 1997.

Wetherby

JONES, BRIAN. *Population listing for the township of Wetherby in the West Riding of Yorkshire, 1776.* Bradford: Brian Jones, 1996. Census compiled by Rev. Richard Kay.

UNWIN, ROBERT. 'An eighteenth-century census: Wetherby, 1776', *Y.A.J.* **54**, 1982, 125-39. Discussion rather than a transcript.

Wortley

FUREY, E.M. 'Wortley inhabitants 1809: a list of the number of inhabitants in the township of Wortley and parish of Tankersley, May 25th 1908', *F.S.* **13**(4), 1993, 99-100; **14**(1), 1993, 17-18; **14**(2), 1993, 48-9; **15**(1), 1994, 18-19; **15**(2), 1994, 45; **15**(3), 1994, 63-5; **15**(4), 1994, 96. The last date given (1908) is a mis-print.

1801

Bracewell

JONES, BRIAN. *1801 census of the township of Bracewell.* Bradford: Brian Jones, 1997.

Elland cum Greetland

SHEASBY, CAROLYN. *Parish of St. John the Baptist, Halifax. Township population books. Elland cum Greetland, 1801.* Hebden Bridge: Calderdale F.H.S., 1992. 1801 census.

Langfield

See under 1811, Sowerby

Leeds

JONES, BRIAN. *1801 census of the parish of Leeds, in the West Riding of Yorkshire.* 2 pts. [Bradford]: Brian Jones, 1996. Pt. 1. East Division, Upper Division. Pt. 2. Mill Hill Division; Kirkgate Division; South Division.

Midgley

SHEASBY, CAROLYN. *Parish of St. John the Baptist Halifax: Midgley township. Population books 1801 and 1811.* Hebden Bridge: Calderdale F.H.S., 1993. Census schedules.

Sandal Magna

JONES, BRIAN. *1801 census of the township of Sandal Magna.* Bradford: Brian Jones, 1999. Not seen.

Thrybergh

JONES, BRIAN. *1801 census of the parish of Thrybergh in the County of Yorkshire.* Bradford: Brian Jones, 1998.

Tong

JONES, BRIAN. *1801 census of the town and lordship of Tong in the parish of Birstall.* Bradford: Brian Jones, 1994.

Calverley and Farsley

JONES, BRIAN. *1811 census of the townships of Calverley and Farsley, in the parish of Calverley.* Bradford: Brian Jones, 1995.

Elland cum Greetland

JONES, BRIAN. *1811 census of the township of Elland cum Greetland in the parish of Halifax.* Bradford: Brian Jones, 1995.

Honley

'Other genealogical sources', *H. & D.F.H.S.J.* 4(1), 1998, 6. Facsimile of an extract from the 1811 census of Honley.

Midgley

See under 1801

Sowerby

SHEASBY, CAROLYN. *Parish of St. John the Baptist, Halifax. Township population books. Sowerby 1811. Langfield 1801.* Hebden Bridge: Calderdale F.H.S., 1993.

Thirsk

JONES, BRIAN. *1811 census of the township of Thirsk in the North Riding of Yorkshire.* Bradford: Brian Jones, 1997.

FIELDHOUSE, R. 'The 1811 census for Thirsk', *Local population studies* 7, 1971, 58-61. Brief note on an early census schedule.

Tong

JONES, BRIAN. *1811 census of the town and lordship of Tong in the parish of Birstall.* Bradford: Brian Jones, 1994.

Yeadon

1811 census of the township of Yeadon in the parish of Guiseley. Bradford: Brian Jones, 1995.

Oswaldkirk

JONES, BRIAN, ed. *1821 census of the township of Oswaldkirk in the North Riding of Yorkshire, also population listing for Castle Bolton in the North Riding of Yorkshire, circa 1880.* Bradford: Brian Jones, 1997.

Spofforth

1821 census of the township of Spofforth in the West Riding of Yorkshire. Bradford: Brian Jones, 1996.

Stansfield

JONES, BRIAN. *1821 census of Stansfield in the parish of Halifax.* 2 pts. Bradford: Brian Jones, 1997.

Thirsk

JONES, BRIAN. *1821 census of the township of Thirsk in the North Riding of Yorkshire.* Bradford: Brian Jones, 1997.

Tong

JONES, BRIAN. *1821 census of the town and lordship of Tong, in the parish of Birstall.* Bradford: Brian Jones, 1997.

Spofforth

JONES, BRIAN. *1831 census for the township of Spofforth in the West Riding of Yorkshire.* Bradford: Brian Jones, 1996.

Almondbury

HUDDERSFIELD & DISTRICT F.H.S. *Almondbury township 1841 census return.* Huddersfield: H. & D.F.H.S., [199-?]

Alwoodley, *etc.*

JONES, BRIAN. *Index of surnames in the 1841 census of the townships of Alwoodley, Harewood, Weardley and Wigton in the parish of Harewood, West Riding of Yorkshire.* Bradford: Brian Jones, 1997.

Bainbridge

ROBERTS, FRED, & ROBERTS, JOYCE. *The township of Bainbridge in the middle of the nineteenth century: the census ennumerators schedules for 1841 & 1851, & the tithe apportionment & map 1844.* N.Y.C.R.O.P. 21. 1979.

Batley

HUDDERSFIELD & DISTRICT FAMILY HISTORY SOCIETY. *Batley township 1841 census return.* 3 pts. Huddersfield: H. & D.F.H.S., [199-?]. Index.

Bingley

1841 census for Bingley and 1851 census for Bingley. Surname index series. Bradford: Bradford F.H.S. 1998. Also available on fiche.

Bradford Area

1841 census for Bradford. 6 vols. Surname index series. Bradford F.H.S., 1997. Also available on fiche. Contents:
- **v.1.** *Bradford, East End.*
- **v.2.** *Bradford, West End.*
- **v.3.** *Horton & Manningham.*
- **v.4.** *Calverley, Idle, & Pudsey.*
- **v.5.** *Bowling, Cleckheaton, & Drightlington.*
- **v.6.** *North Bierley, Thornton & Wilsden.*

Burley and Pool

JONES, BRIAN. *Index of surnames in the 1841 census of Burley and Pool.* Bradford: B. Jones 1996. Not seen.

Calverley cum Farsley, *etc.*

JONES, BRIAN. *Index of surnames in the 1841 census of Calverley cum Farsley, with part of the hamlet of Stanningley.* Bradford: B. Jones, 1996.

Clayton

JONES, BRIAN. *Index of surnames in the 1841 census of Clayton, in the parish of Bradford.* Bradford: B. Jones, 1996.

Clifton cum Hartshead

JONES, BRIAN. *Index of surnames in the 1841 census of Clifton cum Hartshead.* Bradford: Brian Jones, 1996.

Eccleshill

JONES, BRIAN. *Index of surnames in the 1841 census of Eccleshill in the parish of Bradford.* Bradford: B. Jones, 1996.

Fixby

WHITWAM, STEPHEN D., ed. *Kirklees census returns A-Z index. Fixby, 1841, 1851.* Huddersfield: H. & D.F.H.S., 1992.

Fylingdales

'The parish of Fylingdales in 1841: an analysis of census returns', *Journal* 3; N.Y.C.R.O.P. **7**, 1976, 34-76. Lists 402 families.

Golcar

WHITWAM, STEPHEN DAVID. *Golcar township census return, A-Z index 1841.* 2 pts. Huddersfield: H. & D.F.H.S., 1994.

Heckmondwicke

JONES, BRIAN. *Index of surnames in the 1841 census of Heckmondwike.* Bradford: B. Jones, 1996.

Hessay

NEWMAN, P.R. 'The Hessay enclosure of 1831: a study in the economic and social history of an Ainsty township in the 19th century', *Journal* **9**; N.Y.C.R.O.P. **29**, 1982, 89-165. Includes census returns, 1841-71.

Huddersfield

HUDDERSFIELD & DISTRICT FAMILY HISTORY SOCIETY. *Huddersfield Township Census Return, A-Z index, 1841.* 10 pts. Huddersfield: H. & D.F.H.S., 1994.

Ilkley, Baildon and Bramhope

JONES, BRIAN. *Index of surnames in the 1841 census of Ilkley township, Baildon and Bramhope.* Bradford: B. Jones, 1996.

Langtoft

'Some Langtoft households of 1841', *B.T.* **9**, 1981, 11-14. Census schedule.

Meltham

SYKES, DAVID. *Meltham 1841 census returns: index A-[Z].* Huddersfield: H. & D.F.H.S., 1995.

Otley, *etc.*

JONES, BRIAN. *Index of surnames in the 1841 census of Otley Township, Esholt, Hawksworth and Menston.* Bradford: Brian Jones, 1996.

Pocklington

'Some Pocklington households of 1841', *B.T.* **10**, 1981, 7-9. Census schedule.

Saddleworth

FOX, MICHAEL. 'Saddleworth in 1841: a view through the census', *B.S.H.S.* **26**, 1994, 9-22. Includes extracts.

Thornhill

SYKES, DAVID. *Thornhill 1841 census returns index A-Z.* Huddersfield: H. & D.F.H.S., 1995.

Tong and Hunsworth

JONES, BRIAN. *Index of surnames in the 1841 census of Tong and Hunsworth, in the West Riding of Yorkshire.* Bradford: B. Jones, 1996.

Wetherby

JONES, BRIAN. *Index of surnames in the 1841 census of the township of Wetherby.* Bradford: Brian Jones, 1997.

1851
Addingham, *etc.*

1851 census surname index: Addingham, Barden, Beamsley, Bolton Abbey, Drebley, Rylstone, Halton East, Hazelwood/ Storiths, Nesfield & Langbar. Leeds: Wharfedale Family History Group, [1998?]. Not seen.

Adel cum Eccup, *etc.*

LAWSON, GERALD. *1851 census index: Adel cum Eccup, Alwoodley, Arthington, Bardsey, Blubberhouses, Castley, Dunkeswick, Fewston, Great Timble, Harewood, Little Timble, Norwood, Rigton, Weardley, Weeton, Wigton & Wike.* Leeds: Wharfedale Family History Group, 1997.

Almondbury

WHITWAM, STEPHEN DAVID, & WHITWAM, DIANE. *Kirklees census returns, A-[Z] index. Almondbury, 1851.* 4 vols. Huddersfield: H. & D.F.H.S., 1990.

Appletreewick, *etc.*

1851 census surname index: Appletreewick, Arncliffe, Beckermonds, Bordley, Buckden, Burnsall, Conistone, Cracoe, Foxup, Grassington, Halton Gill, Harlington, Hawkswick, Linton, Litton, Outershaw, Starbottom, Thorpe, Threshfield & Yockenthwaite. Leeds: Wharfedale Family History Group, 1998.

Askwith, *etc.*

LAWSON, GERALD. *1851 census index Askwith, Burley in Wharfedale, Denton, Ilkley, Middleton & Weston.* Leeds: Wharfedale Family History Group, 1997.

Austonley

WHITWAM, STEPHEN D. *Kirklees census returns, A-Z index. Austonley, 1851.* Huddersfield: H. & D.F.H.S., 1990.

Baildon, *etc.*

HOLMES, LESLEY A., ed. *1851 census index: Baildon with Esholt and Hawkesworth.* Occasional paper **14.** Leeds: Y.A.S., F.H.P.S.S., 1992.

WARREN, ANDREW. 'More Keighley & district strays', *K.D.F.H.S.J.* Winter 1993, 10-11. From 1851 census for Baildon.

Barnsley Area

BARNSLEY F.H.S. *Index to 1851 census.* Barnsley: Barnsley F.H.S., 1992- . Contents:
v.1. *Silkstone.*
v.2. *Thurgoland & Crane Moor.*
v.3. *Penistone & Langsett.*
v.4. *Cawthorne.*
v.5. *Rexborough.*
v.6. *Oxspring & Hunshelf.*
v.7. *Tankersley & Pilley.*
v.8. *Hoylandswaine, Gunthwaite & Ingbirchworth.*
v.9. *Darfield, with Great Houghton, Little Houghton, and Billingley.*
v.10. *Wombwell & Hemingfield.*
v.11. *Monk Bretton.*
v.12. *Thurlestone.*
v.13. *Ardsley.*
v.14. *Worsborough.*
v.15. *Barnsley town centre (forthcoming).*

Batley

BRUCE, STEVEN F. *Kirklees census returns index A-Z. Batley, 1851.* 4 vols. Huddersfield: H. & D.F.H.S., 1988.
'Extract of Batley 1851 census: the Workhouse', *Cameo* 1991, no.2, 14.

Bishopton

DENTON, JEAN. 'Census abstracts: the population of Bishopston 1851-1861', *R.H.* **1**(2), 1988, 12-15. General discussion.

Bradfield
1861 census index: Chapelry of Bradfield. 2 pts. Sheffield: Sheffield & District F.H.S., 1990-91.

Bradford Moor
KENZIE, K. 'Bradford Moor barracks: census 1851', *Bod-Kin* **20**, 1990, 10-12.

Bramham, *etc.*
1851 census index: Bramham, Thorp Arch, Newton Kyme, Ulleskelf, Kirkby Wharfe, Stutton Healaugh, and Wighill. Occasional paper **27**. Leeds Y.A.S., F.H.P.S.S., 1996.

Bramhope, *etc.*
LAWSON, GERALD. *1851 census index: Bramhope, Farnley, Leathley, Lindley, Menston, Newall with Clifton, Pool in Wharfedale, & Stainburn.* Leeds: Wharfedale Family History Group, 1997.

Bramley with Stanningley
HOLMES, LESLEY A., ed. *1851 census index: Bramley with Stanningley.* Occasional paper **12**. Leeds: Y.A.S., F.H.P.S.S., 1992.

Bridlington Area
EAST YORKSHIRE FAMILY HISTORY SOCIETY. *Index to 1851 census: H0107/2367: Bridlington district.* [ ]: E.Y.F.H.S., 1993.
EAST YORKSHIRE FAMILY HISTORY SOCIETY. *Index to 1851 census H0107/2367 fol. 80v-258: Bridlington and Bridlington Quay* [ ]: E.Y.F.H.S., [199-?]

Broughton
'1851 census, Broughton', *K.D.F.H.S.J.* Winter 1994, 21. Surnames only.
The 1851 census index for Broughton, Carlton, Elslack, Lothersdale and Stirton with Thirlby. Keighley: Keighley & District F.H.S., 1999. Not seen.

Burton Constable
GLENTON, C. '1851 census: Burton Constable Hall', *B.T.* **26**, 1986, 7-10. On the night of a party!

Calverley, Farsley & Pudsey
HOLMES, LESLEY A., ed. *1851 census index: Calverley, Farsley and Pudsey (East), part I.* Occasional paper **5**. Leeds: Y.A.S., F.H.P.S.S., 1987.

Cartworth
WHITWAM, STEPHEN D. *Kirklees census returns, A-Z index. Cartworth 1851.* Huddersfield: H. & D.F.H.S., 1992.

Catwick
'Some Catwick households of 1851', *B.T.* **9**, 1980/1, 12-16. Census schedule; includes list of names on gravestones.

Cherry Burton
'Some old Cherry Burton households of 1851: census returns 1851, Cherry Burton, north side of Town Street, east to west', *B.T.* **6**, 1980, 14-17.

Clayton West & High Hoyland
WHITWAM, STEPHEN DAVID. *Kirklees census returns, A-Z index. Clayton West and High Hoyland 1857.* Huddersfield: H. & D.F.H.S., 1991.

Cleckheaton
WHITWAM, STEPHEN D., ed. *Kirklees census returns, A-Z index. Cleckheaton 1851.* 2 vols. Huddersfield: H. & D.F.H.S., 1992.

Cleveland
CLEVELAND FAMILY HISTORY SOCIETY. *1851 census for ..* Yarm: C.F.H.S., 1982-96. Contents (volumes not listed here relate to Co.Durham):
v.2. *High Worsall, Kirkleighton, Stainton, West Acklam, & Linthorpe.*
v.3. *Yarm.*
v.4. *Thornaby.*
v.5. *Easington; Brotton.*
v.6. *Skelton.*
v.7. *Loftus.*
v.8. *Kirkleatham; Upleatham.*
v.9. *Redcar; Marske.*
v.10. *Great Ayton; Little Ayton.*
v.11. *Billingham, Claxton, Cowpen Bewley, Greatham, Haverton Hill, Newton Bewley, Port Clarence, Wolviston.*
v.13. *Wilton, Ormesby, Cleveland Part, Eston & Normanby.*
v.18. *Guisborough.*
v.19. *Hemlington, Hilton, Marton, Nunthorpe, Tollesby.*

v.21. Deighton, East and West Harlsey, East and South Cowton, Hutton Bonville, Birkby, Little Smeaton.

v.23. Commondale, Castleton, Danby and Westerdale.

v.24. Northallerton and Romanby.

v.25. Stokesley.

v.26. Faceby, Hutton Rudby, Seamer, Middleton on Leven, Sexhow, Potto, Ingelby Cross, Ingelby Arncliffe, Crathorne.

v.27. Fylingdales.

v.28. Hinderwell, Staithes, Roxby, Runswick Bay.

v.29. Newby, Easby, Carlton, Kildale, Whorlton.

v.31. Barnby, Kettleness, Borrowby, Lythe, Ellerby, Mickleby, Goldsbrough, Sandsend, Mulgrave, Ugthorpe.

v.34. Sleights, Eskdaleside, Glaisdale.

v.35. Ellerbeck, Nether Silton, Over Silton, Thimbleby, Osmotherley.

v.36. Ruswarp.

v.37. Whitby. (2 pts).

v.38. Egton, Ugglebarnby, Goathland.

v.39. Brompton (Northallerton), Kirby Sigston, Thornton le Beans.

v.40. Ingleby Greenhow, Battersby, Kirby and Dromonby, Busby, Scutterskelfe, Great and Little Broughton.

v.42. Newholm cum Dunsley, Sneaton, Aislaby, Hawsker cum Stainsacre.

v.47. Croft, Enryholme, Dalton, Sockburn, Girsby, Dinsdale, Over Dinsdale.

v.48. Manfield, Cliffe, Cleasby, Stapleton, Blackwell, Barton, Oxneyfield, Newton Morrell.

v.54. Landmoth with Catto and Gueldable, Barrowby, Crosby, Leake, Cotcliffe, Sowerby under Cotcliffe, Winton with Stank, North Otterington with Warlaby.

v.55. Thirsk.

v.56. Thornton le Street, Thornton le Moor, North Kilvington, Knayton, Kepwick, Cowesby.

v.57. Richmond.

v.59. Ainderby Quernhow, Catton, Sinderby, Skipton, Howe, Holme, Pickhill with Roxby.

v.62. Ainderby Steeple, Morton on Swale, Thrintoft, Yafforth, Danby Wiske with Lazenby, Great and Little Langton, Whitwell, Kiplin.

v.63. Hutton Sessay, Birdforth, Sessay, Dalton, Eldmine, Fawdington, Topcliffe.

v.64. Sowerby.

v.65. South Kilvington, Bagby, Sutton with Balk, Thirkleby.

v.66. Barforth, Ovington, Wycliffe, Hutton Magna, Barningham, Scargill, Hope.

v.67. Kilburn, Felixkirk, Thirlby, Boltby, Upsall Thornborough, Kirkby Knowle.

v.68. Maunby, Newby Wiske, South Otterington, Kirby Wiske, Newsham cum Breckenbrough, Carlton Miniott, Sandhutton.

v.69. Coniscliffe, Carlbury, Piercebridge, Cockerton, Archdeacon Newton, Coldsides, Houghton le Side, Denton, Summerhouses.

v.70. Downholme, Stainton, Walburne, Marske, Hudswell, Hipswell, Easby, Aske.

v.71. Skeeby, Gilling, Hartforth, Gatherley Moor, Sedbury.

v.72. Catterick, Brough, Scotton, Colburn, Tunstall, Appleton, Ellerton, Bolton on Swale, Scorton.

v.73. Brignall, Rokeby, Boldron, Bowes, Streatlam, Stainton, Marwood.

v.74. Gilmonby, Whorlton, Westwick, Eggleston Abbey, Startforth.

v.77. Middleton Tyas with North Cowton, Moulton Uckerby, Brompton on Swale.

v.78. Aldbrough and Stanwick, Eppleby, Melsonby.

v.81. Kirby Hill with Whashton, Ravensworth, Gayles, New Forest.

v.84. Lartington, Cotherstone, Hunderthwaite, Romaldkirk, Mickleton, Lunedale, Holwick. (2 pts).

v.85. Killerby, Kirby Fleetham, Fencote, Ainderby cum Holtby, Scruton, Firby.

v.86. Bedale.

v.87. Gatenby, Swainby, Theakston, Burneston, Carthorpe, Kirklington.

v.88. Well, Snape, Thornton Watlass.

25

v.89. *Hawnby, Bilsdale West Side, Dale Town and Morton, Arden and Snilesworth, Old Byland, Helmsley and Carlton, Rivaulx and Laskill, Bilsdale Midcable, Beadlam.*

v.90. *Packley, Harum, Sproxton, Scawton and Cold Kirby, Oldstead & Wass & Thorpe le Willows, Byland Abbey, Ampleforth and Birdforth, Oswaldkirk & West Newton Grange, Oswaldkirk Quarter, Ampleforth College.*

v.91. *Cawton and Grimston, Coulton, East Ness and Nunnington, Edstone Great, Little and North Holme, Gilling East, Muscoates and Welburn, Normanby, Thornton Risebrough, Salton, Stonegrave and East Newton, Wombleton.*

v.92. *Nawton, Bransdale and Skiplam, Farndale West Side, Gillamoor, Fadmoor, Hutton le Hole, Farndale East Side.*

v.93. *Kirbymoorside, Appleton le Moor.*

v.94. (a.) *Aysgarth, Carperby & Thoralby, Burton cum Walden, Newbiggin, Bishopdale.*

v.94. (b.) *Thoralby, Thornton Rust, Bainbridge.*

v.95. *Askrigg, Abbotside, Burtersett.*

v.96. *Reeth, Healaugh, Raw and Castle, Fremington, Whitaside, Harkerside, Grinton.*

v.97. *Arkengarthdale, Hurst, Marrick, Ellerton Abbey.*

v.98. *Gayle, Hawes, Appersett.*

v.99. *Thorns and Keld, Stonesdale and Birkdale, Angram and Agill, Thwaite, Muker, Oxnop and Satron, Ivelet.*

v.100. *Gunnerside, Lodge Green, Melbecks, Low Row, Kearton, Feetham.*

v.101. *Firby, Langthorn, Leeming and Newton, Londonderry, Exelby.*

v.102. *Masham, Swinton, Ilton cum Pott.*

v.103. *Crakehall, Aiskew and Leeming Bar.*

v.104. *Healey and Sutton, Fearby, Ellingtons, Ellingstring, East Witton, Colsterdale.*

v.105. *Middleham.*

v.106. *Dalton, W. Layton, Newsham, E. Layton, Carkin, Caldwell, Forcett.*

v.107. *Coverham, Caldbergh, West Scrafton, Calton, (Highdale), Melmerby, West Witton.*

v.108. *Wensley, Preston, Redmire, Castle Bolton, Leyburn and (Workhouse).*

v.109. *Spennithorne, Bellerby, Hawkswell, Garriston with Barden, Hornby, Hunton.*

v.110. *Newton le Willows, Burrell, Burton on Ure, Thirn, Thornton Steward, Fingall, Constable Burton.*

v.112. *Pickering.*

v.116. *Lastingham, Rosedale East and West, Cropton Hartoft, Cawthorne, Aislaby, Middleton.*

v.117. *Newton, Marishes, Sinnington, Marton, Kirby Misterton, Great Barugh, Little Barugh, Thornton Dale.*

v.118. *Farmanby, Wilton, Allerston, Ebberston, Lockton, Levisham.*

Cottingham, *etc.*

EAST YORKSHIRE FAMILY HISTORY SOCIETY. *Index to 1851 census: H0107/2360 fol. 246-520v. Cottingham, North Ferriby, Hessle & District.* Cottingham: E.Y.F.H.S., 1996.

Cumberworth

OGDEN, JANET, ed. *Kirklees census return A-[Z] index, Cumberworth and Cumberworth Half, 1851.* 2 vols. Huddersfield: H. & D.F.H.S., 1989.

Dalton

WHITWAM, STEPHEN DAVID & WHITWAM, DIANE, eds. *Kirklees census returns, A-[Z] index. Dalton 1851.* 2 vols. Huddersfield: H. & D.F.H.S., 1991.

Denby

WHITWAM, STEPHEN DAVID, & WHITWAM, DIANE, eds. *Kirklees census returns, A-Z index. Denby, 1851.* Huddersfield: H. & D.F.H.S., 1991.

Dewsbury

WHITWAM, STEPHEN D., ed. *Kirklees census returns, A-[Z] index, Dewsbury 1851.* 5 vols. Huddersfield: H. & D.F.H.S., 1992.

Doncaster Area

Index to 1851 census. [Doncaster]: Doncaster Society for Family History, 1981-97.

Draughton & Elslack

'1851 census: Draughton & Elslack', *K.D.F.H.S.J.* Autumn 1994, 23. Surnames only.

Driffield

EAST YORKSHIRE F.H.S. *Index to 1851 census: H0107/2366 fol. 4v-381 [& 385v-650v.] Driffield and district.* 2 vols. Cottingham: E.Y.F.H.S., 1996.

Easington

MOUNT, DAVID. 'Easington', *B.T.* **16,** 1983, 10-12. Includes surnames on inscriptions, extracts from an 1840 directory, and 1851 census (part).

East Sculcoates

EAST YORKSHIRE F.H.S. *Index to 1851 census: H0107/2361 fol. 4v-363v. East Sculcoates* 2 vols. [ ]: E.Y.F.H.S., [199-?]

Emley

WHITWAM, STEPHEN DAVID, ed. *Kirklees census returns, A-Z index. Emley 1851.* Huddersfield: H. & D.F.H.S., 1990.

Farnley Tyas

WHITWAM, STEPHEN DAVID, & WHITWAM, DIANE. *Kirklees census returns, A-Z index. Farnley Tyas 1851.* Huddersfield: H. & D.F.H.S., 1991.

Fulstone

WHITWAM, STEPHEN D., ed. *Kirklees census return A-Z index. Fulstone 1851.* Huddersfield: H. & D.F.H.S., 1990.

Fylingdales

FYLINGDALES LOCAL HISTORY GROUP.
Fylingdales census return 1851 & 1861.
N.Y.C.R.O.P. **20**. 1979.

Garforth, *etc.*

1851 census index: Garforth, Kippax, Great & Little Preston, South Milford.
Occasional paper **29**. Leeds: Y.A.S.,
F.H.P.S.S., 1997.

Garsdale, *etc.*

Transcript & index for the 1851 census for Garsdale, Dent and Kirkthwaite (H0107/2276; folios 88 to 182). [ ]:
Cumbria F.H.S., 1996.

Golcar

WHITWAM, STEPHEN D., ed. *Kirklees census returns, A-Z index: Golcar, 1851.*
2 vols. Huddersfield: H. & D.F.H.S.,
1988.

Gomersal

WHITWAM, STEPHEN DAVID., ed. *Kirklees census returns, A-[Z] index. Gomersal, 1851.* 4 vols. Huddersfield: H. & D.F.H.S.,
1992.

Guisborough

1851 census index of Guisborough, H0107/2375. 3 fiche. [ ]: Cleveland F.H.S.,
[199-?].

Guiseley with Carlton

HOLMES, LESLEY A., ed. *1851 census index: Guiseley with Carlton.* Occasional paper
13. Leeds: Y.A.S., F.H.P.S.S., 1992.

Halifax and Skircoat

RYCROFT, N., et al. '1851 census returns for Halifax and Skircoat townships',
T.Hal.A.S. 1979, 105-23.; 1981, 39-69.
Sociological analysis; *not* a transcript.

Harewood

JONES, BRIAN. *Index of surnames in the 1841 census of the townships of Dunkeswick, Weeton, East Keswick, and Wike, in the parish of Harewood, West Riding of Yorkshire.* Bradford: Brian Jones, 1997.

Harrogate Area

Index to 1851 census. 7 vols. [Harrogate]:
Harrogate Family History Society, [199-].
Contents:

  v.1. *Parishes of Aldborough (inc. Boroughbridge), Copgrove, Marton cum Grafton, Ripley, & Staveley.*
  v.2. *Parishes of Hampsthwaite and Pannal (including Low Harrogate), and townships of Kirkby Overblow and Follifoot.*
  v.3. *Bilton with Harrogate.*
  v.4-5. *Knaresborough and Scriven.*
  v.6. *Parishes of Farnham, Goldsborough, Great Ouseburn, Little Ouseburn, Kirk Hammerton, Nidd, Nun Monkton and Whixley, with parts of Hunsingore, Knaresbro and Spofforth.*
  v.7. *Parishes of Allerton Mauleverer, Cowthorpe, Hunsingore, Kirkby Overblow (part), Kirk Deighton & Spofforth (inc. Wetherby).*

'Keighley & district strays found on the 1851 census for Harrogate', *K.D.F.H.S.J.*
Autumn 1995, 5.

Hartshead cum Clifton

WHITWAM, STEPHEN D., ed. *Kirklees census returns, A-Z index. Hartshead cum Clifton 1851.* Huddersfield: H. & D.F.H.S., 1992.

Headingley cum Birley

HOLMES, LESLEY A., ed. *1851 census index: Headingley cum Birley.* Occasional paper
16. Leeds: Y.A.S., F.H.P.S.S., 1992.

Hebden Bridge

RALPH, NORMAN, & RALPH, ANGELA. *1851 census transcript & surname index: Hebden Bridge, Yorkshire.* 5 fiche.
Hebden Bridge: Calderdale F.H.S., [199-?].

Heckmondwike

WHITWAM, STEPHEN DAVID., ed. *Kirklees census returns, A-[Z] index: Heckmondwike, 1851.* 2 vols. Huddersfield:
H. & D.F.H.S., 1993.

Hedon, Drypool & District

EAST YORKSHIRE F.H.S., *Index to 1851 census: H0107/2360, fol. 521-765v. (end). Hedon, Drypool & district (includes Hull Garrison).* Cottingham: E.Y.F.H.S., 1996.

Helmsley

Helmsley 1851 census index. 2 fiche. [ ]: Cleveland ... F.H.S., [199-].

Hepworth

OGDEN, JANET. *Kirklees census returns, A-Z index. Hepworth 1851.* Huddersfield: H. & D.F.H.S., 1989.

Hessay

See 1841

Holbeck, Beeston & Churwell

HOLMES, LESLEY A., ed. *1851 census index: Holbeck, Beeston & Churwell.* Occasional paper **6**. Leeds: Y.A.S., F.H.P.S.S., 1987.

Holme

WHITWAM, STEPHEN DAVID, ed. *Kirklees census returns, A-Z index. Holme, 1851.* Huddersfield: H. & D.F.H.S., 1991.

Holme on Spalding Moor, *etc*.

EAST YORKSHIRE F.H.S., *Index to 1851 census H0107/2358, fol. 4v. 108. Holme on Spalding Moor, Bubwith, Aughton area.* Cuttingham: E.Y.F.H.S., 1984. Superseded by index to Howden Registration District (see below)

Honley

WHITWAM, STEPHEN DAVID, & WHITWAM, DIANE, eds. *Kirklees census returns, A-[Z] index: Honley, 1851.* 2 vols. Huddersfield: H. & D.F.H.S., 1992.

Horsforth

HOLMES, LESLEY A., ed. *1851 census index: Horsforth.* Occasional paper **15**. Leeds: Y.A.S., F.H.P.S.S., 1992.

Howden District

EAST YORKSHIRE F.H.S. *Index to 1851 census: H0107/2358. Howden district.* 2 vols. Cottingham: E.Y.F.H.S., 1994.

Huddersfield

WHITWAM, STEPHEN D., & WHITWAM, DIANE, eds. *Kirklees census returns, A-[Z] index. Huddersfield 1851.* 11 vols. Huddersfield: H. & D.F.H.S., 1990-93.

Hull

EAST YORKSHIRE F.H.S., *Index to 1851 census: H0107/2363. Holy Trinity, Hull.* 3 vols in 6. Cottingham: E.Y.F.H.S., 1991-2.

Hunslet

HOLMES, LESLEY A., ed. *1851 census index: Hunslet.* 2 vols. Occasional paper **10**. Leeds: Y.A.S., F.H.P.S.S., 1989.

Hunsworth

WHITWAM, STEPHEN DAVID, & WHITWAM, DIANE, eds. *Kirklees census returns, A-Z index. Hunsworth, 1851.* Huddersfield: H. & D.F.H.S., 1991.

Kirkburton

WHITWAM, STEPHEN DAVID, ed. *Kirklees census returns, A-[Z] index. Kirkburton 1851.* 2 vols. Huddersfield: H. & D.F.H.S., 1990.

Kirkheaton

WHITWAM, STEPHEN D., ed. *Kirklees census returns, A-Z index. Kirkheaton, 1851.* Huddersfield: H. & D.F.H.S., 1990.

Kirkstall

HOLMES, LESLEY A., ed. *1851 census index: Kirkstall.* Occasional paper **18**. Leeds: Y.A.S., F.H.P.S.S., 1993.

Lepton

WHITWAM, STEPHEN DAVID, ed. *Kirklees census returns, A-[Z] index. Lepton 1851.* 2 vols. Huddersfield: H. & D.F.H.S., 1991.

Lindley cum Quarmby

ELLIFE, CHARLES. *Kirklees census returns A-[Z] index. Lindley cum Quarmby, 1851.* 2 vols. Huddersfield: H. & D.F.H.S., 1989.

Lingards

Kirklees census returns, A-Z index. Lingards, 1851. Huddersfield: H. & D.F.H.S., 1988.

Linthwaite

WHITWAM, STEPHEN DAVID, & WHITWAM, DIANE, eds. *Kirklees census returns, A-Z index. Linthwaite 1851.* 2 vols. Huddersfield: H. & D.F.H.S., 1990.

Liversedge

WHITWAM, STEPHEN DAVID, ed. *Kirklees census returns. A-[Z] index. Liversedge 1851.* 3 vols. Huddersfield: H. & D.F.H.S., 1992.

Lockwood

WHITWAM, STEPHEN DAVID, & WHITWAM, DIANE, eds. *Kirklees census returns A-[Z] index. Lockwood 1851.* 2 vols. Huddersfield: H. & D.F.H.S., 1990.

Longwood

WHITWAM, STEPHEN D., ed. *Kirklees census returns A-Z index. Longwood 1851.* Huddersfield: H. & D.F.H.S., 1990.

Lower & Upper Whitley

WHITWAM, STEPHEN DAVID, ed. *Kirklees census returns, A-Z index. Lower and Upper Whitley 1851.* Huddersfield: H. & D.F.H.S., 1992.

Marsden

WHITWAM, STEPHEN D., ed. *Kirklees census returns, A-Z index. Marsden 1851.* Huddersfield: H. & D.F.H.S., 1990.

Meltham

WHITWAM, STEPHEN D., ed. *Kirklees census returns, A-[Z] index. Meltham, 1851.* 2 vols. Huddersfield: H. & D.F.H.S., 1992.

Middleton on the Wolds

'Middleton-on-the-Wolds: 1851 census', *B.T.* **11**, 1981, 8-10. Census schedule.

Mirfield

WHITWAM, STEPHEN DAVID, ed. *Kirklees census returns, A-[Z] index. Mirfield 1851.* 3 vols. Huddersfield: H. & D.F.H.S., 1992.

Morley & Batley

HOLMES, LESLEY A., ed. *1851 census index: Morley and Batley.* Occasional paper **11**. 2 vols. Leeds: Y.A.S., F.H.P.S.S., 1989.

Naburn, Escrick & Dunningham

EAST YORKSHIRE F.H.S. *Index to 1851 census: H0107/2356 folio 4v-157. Ouse & Derwent area Naburn, Escrick, Dunnington.* Cottingham: E.Y.F.H.S., 1994.

Netherthong

WHITWAM, STEPHEN D., ed. *Kirklees census returns. A-Z index. Netherthong 1851.* Huddersfield: H. & D.F.H.S., 1992.

North Newbald

'Some North Newbald households of 1851', *B.T.* **7**, 1980, 14-19. Census schedule.

Otley

LAWSON, GERALD. *1851 census index Otley.* 2 vols. Leeds: Wharfedale Family History Group, 1997.

Patrington Area

EAST YORKSHIRE FAMILY HISTORY SOCIETY. *Index to 1851 census. H0107/2364. Patrington and district.* Hull: E.Y.F.H.S., [199-?].

Pickering

Pickering 1851 census index. 3 fiche. Cleveland, N. Yorks & S. Durham F.H.S., 1993.

Potter Newton & Chapel Allerton

HOLMES, LESLEY A., ed. *1851 census index: Potter Newton and Chapel Allerton.* Occasional paper **17**. Y.A.S., F.H.P.S.S., 1993.

Pudsey with Tyersall

HOLMES, LESLEY A., ed. *1851 census index: Pudsey (West) with Tyersall (part 2).* Occasional paper **9**. Leeds: Y.A.S., F.H.P.S.S., 1998.

Rawdon

HOLMES, LESLEY, ed. *1851 census index: Rawdon.* Occasional paper **20**. Leeds: Y.A.S., F.H.P.S.S., 1994.

Rothwell

HOLMES, LESLEY A., ed. *1851 census index: Rothwell.* Occasional paper **22**. Leeds: Y.A.S., F.H.P.S.S., 1994.

Scammonden

WHITWAM, STEPHEN DAVID., ed. *Kirklees census returns. A-Z index. Scammonden, 1851.* Huddersfield, H. & D.F.H.S., 1989.

Scarborough District

EAST YORKSHIRE FAMILY HISTORY SOCIETY. *Index to 1851 census H0107/2368 fol. 14-125, 5.12-830. Scarborough district (exc. town).* 2 vols. Cottingham: E.Y.F.H.S., 1990. The full title is not printed on the 2nd volume; hence it omits all reference to the fact that it is an index to the 1851 census.

EAST YORKSHIRE FAMILY HISTORY SOCIETY. *Index to 1851 Cenus H0107/2368, fol. 129v-509v. Scarborough.* 2 vols. Cottingham: E.Y.F.H.S., 1995.

Shadwell, *etc.*

HOLMES, LESLEY A., ed. *1851 census index: Shadwell, Roundhay, and Seacroft.* Occasional paper **21**. Leeds: Y.A.S., F.H.P.S.S., 1994.

Shelley

OGDEN, JANET. *Kirklees census returns A-Z index. Shelley 1851.* Huddersfield: H. & D.F.H.S., 1988.

Shepley

OGDEN, JANET, ed. *Kirklees census returns A-Z index. Shepley, 1851.* Huddersfield: H. & D.F.H.S, 1988.

Skirlaugh District

EAST YORKSHIRE YORKSHIRE FAMILY HISTORY SOCIETY. *Index to the 1851 census. H0107/2365. Skirlaugh and district.* Cottingham: E.Y.F.H.S., 1993.

Slaithwaite

WHITWAM, STEPHEN D., & WHITWAM, DIANE, eds. *Kirklees census returns, A-Z index. Slaithwaite, 1851.* Huddersfield: H. & D.F.H.S., 1990.

South Crosland

WHITWAM, STEPHEN DAVID, ed *Kirklees census returns, A-Z index. South Crosland, 1851.* Huddersfield: H. & D.F.H.S., 1992.

Sutton on Hull & District

EAST YORKSHIRE FAMILY HISTORY SOCIETY. *Index to 1851 census H0107/2360 fol 4v-245. Sutton on Hull & District.* Cottingham: E.Y.F.H.S., 1995.

Soothill

WHITWAM, STEPHEN DAVID, ed. *Kirklees census returns, A-[Z] index, Soothill 1851.* 2 vols. Huddersfield: H. & D.F.H.S., 1992.

South Dalton

'South Dalton', *B.T.* **18**, 1984, 10-11. Census 1851; also includes extract from Baines' *directory,* 1823 and brief list of names on gravestones.

Southport (Lancashire)

WRIGHT, C., 'Southport census of 1851 (Yorkshire born residents & visitors)', *H. & D.F.H.S.J.* **9**(3), 1996, 20-21.

Swine

MOUNT, DAVID. '1851 census returns for Swine', *B.T.* **13**, 1982, 10-11.

Tadcaster Area

1851 census index: Tadcaster, Bilbrough, Bickerton, Bilton, Tockwith, Long Marston, etc. Occasional paper 28. Y.A.S., F.H.P.S.S., 1996. Also available on fiche.

Thirsk

1851 census index: Thirsk area. 2 fiche. [ ]: Cleveland ... F.H.S., 1993.

Thornhill

WHITWAM, STEPHEN DAVID, & WHITWAM, DIANE, eds. *Kirklees census returns, A-Z index. Thornhill 1851.* Huddersfield: H. & D.F.H.S., 1991.

Thurstonland

WHITWAM, STEPHEN DAVID, & WHITWAM, DIANE, eds. *Kirklees census returns, A-Z index. Thurstonland 1851.* Huddersfield: H. & D.F.H.S., 1992.

Upperthong

WHITWAM, STEPHEN DAVID, ed. *Kirklees census returns, A-Z index. Upperthong, 1851.* Huddersfield: H. & D.F.H.S., 1992.

Wakefield Area

Index to 1851 census. Wakefield: Wakefield and District F.H.S., 1997-8.
v. 1-7. *Wakefield.*
v.8. *Wakefield Prison.*

v.9. *Ackworth and Ackworth School.*

v.10-12. *Alverthorpe with Thornes.*

v.13. *Badsworth, Darrington, Thorp Audlin, and Upton.*

v.14. *Castleford & Glass Houghton.*

v.15. *Crigglestone.*

v.16. *Crofton, Heath, Sharlstone & Warmfield.*

v.17. *Aketon, Whitwood, Featherstone and Purston Jaglin.*

v.18. *Felkirk, Havercroft, Ryhill, South Hiendley and Wintersett.*

v.19. *Ferrybridge and Ferry Fryston.*

v.20. *Hemsworth.*

v.21-2. *Horbury.*

v.23-4. *Knottingley.*

v.25. *Altofts, Normanton and Snydale.*

v.26-8. *Ossett.*

v.29-31. *Pontefract, Carlton & East Hardwick.*

v.32. *Chevet, West Bretton, Notton & Woolley.*

v.33. *Sandal Magna and Walton.*

v.34. *North Elmsall, South Elmsall and South Kirby*

v.35-8. *Stanley with Wrenthorpe.*

v.39. *Middlestown, Midgley, Netherton and Overton.*

v.40. *Wragby, West Hardwick, Foulby with Nostell and Ryhill.*

West Sculcoates

EAST YORKSHIRE FAMILY HISTORY SOCIETY. *Index to 1851 census H0107/2361, fol. 379v.-725. West Sculcoates.* 2 vols. Cottingham: E.Y.F.H.S., [199-?].

Wooldale

WHITWAM, STEPHEN D., & WHITWAM, DIANE, eds. *Kirklees census returns, A-[Z] index. Wooldale, 1851.* 2 vols. Huddersfield: H. & D.F.H.S., 1990.

Wortley, *etc.*

HOLMES, LESLEY A., ed. *1851 census index: Wortley, Farnley, Armley & Gildersome.* Occasional paper **8.** Leeds: Y.A.S., F.H.P.S.S., 1998.

Yeadon

HOLMES, LESLEY, ed. *1851 census index: Yeadon.* Occasional paper **19.** Leeds: Y.A.S., F.H.P.S.S., 1993.

1861

Askrigg

'Yorkshire strays born outside Wensleydale in Askrigg census returns', *Y.F.H.* **21**(1), 1995, 19. For 1861.

Bingley

1861 census for Bingley and 1871 census for Bingley. Surname index series. Bradford: Bradford F.H.S., 1998.

Bradfield

SHEFFIELD & DISTRICT FAMILY HISTORY SOCIETY. *1861 census index: Chapelry of Bradfield.* 2 vols. Sheffield: The Society, 1990-91.

Hessay

See 1841

Horsforth

1861 census index. Horsforth. Leeds: Wharfedale Family History Group, 1998.

Sheffield Area

SHEFFIELD & DISTRICT FAMILY HISTORY SOCIETY. *1861 Census Index, Sheffield.* 45 vols. Sheffield: Sheffield & District F.H.S., 1987- . Vols 12-24 only available on fiche. Contents:

v.1-4. *Sheffield West.*

v.5-11. *Sheffield North.*

v. 12-14. *Sheffield South.*

v.15-18. *Sheffield Park.*

v.19-24. *Brightside.*

v.25-7. *Attercliffe cum Darnall; Handsworth and Beighton.*

v. 28-32. *Nether Hallam and Upper Hallam.*

v. 33-41. *Ecclesall; Bierlow.*

v.42-44. *Ecclesfield.*

v.45. *Rotherham.*

1871

Adel, *etc.*

1871 census index: Adel, Alwoodley, Arthington, Bramhope, Dunkeswick, Eccup, North Rigton, Pool & Weeton. Leeds: Wharfedale Family History Group, [1998?]. Not seen.

Bingley

See 1861

Blubberhouses, *etc.*
1871 census index: Blubberhouses, Fewston, Lindley, Norwood & Timble. Leeds: Wharfedale Family History Group, [1998?] Not seen.

Bradford Area
1871 Bradford census surnames index. 9 vols. Bradford: Bradford F.H.S., 1994. Contents:
1-2. *Sub-district of Bradford, East End.*
v.3. *Sub-district of Bradford, West End.*
v. 4-5. *Sub-district of Horton.*
v.6. *Sub-district of Bowling and North Bierley.*
v.7. *Sub-district of Thornton, Wilsden & Shipley.*
v.8. *Sub-districts of Idle, Calverley, & Pudsey.*
v.9. *Sub-districts of Cleckheaton and Drightlington.*

Harewood, *etc.*
1871 census index: Harewood, Weardley, Leathley, Castley, Stainburn, Farnley, Newall with Clifton. Leeds: Wharfedale Family History Group, [1998?]. Not seen.

Hessay
See 1841

Horsforth
LAWSON, GERALD. *1871 census index: Horsforth.* Leeds: Wharfedale Family History Group, 1997.

Ilkley
LAWSON, GERALD. *1871 census index: Ilkley.* Leeds: Wharfedale Family History Group, 1998.

Otley
1871 census index: Otley. 2 pts. Leeds: Wharfedale Family History Group, [1998?]

Rawdon
1871 census index: Rawdon. Leeds: Wharfedale Family History Group, 1998.

Shipley
'1871 census, Shipley, Yorkshire', *Wh. N.* **23**, 1997, 14-15. List of Wharfedale strays.

Yeadon & Hawksworth
1871 census index: Yeadon & Hawksworth. Leeds: Wharfedale Family History Group, [1998?]. Not seen.

1881
1881 census surname index, county: Yorkshire. Many fiche. [ ]: Federation of Family History Societies, 1992. Comprehensive.

York
SLATER, IRIS. 'Away from home on census night, 1881', *C.Y.D.F.H.S.J.* **35**, 1995, 7-8. Census return for York County Hospital, Monkgate.

1891
Portland (Dorset)
BLAKESTON, MICHAEL. 'Portland, Dorset, strays', *B.T.* **76**, 1998, 25-6. From Yorkshire, 1891 census.

Bingley
1891 census index for Bingley. Surname index series. [Bradford]: Bradford F.H.S. 1996.

Bradford Area
BRADFORD FAMILY HISTORY SOCIETY. *1891 census for Bradford. Surname index series.* 11 vols. Bradford: B.F.H.S., 1992. Contents:
v.1-2. *Sub-district of Bradford, East End.*
v.3-4. *Sub-district of Bradford, West End.*
v.5-6. *Sub-district of Horton.*
v.7. *Sub-district of Bowling.*
v.8. *Sub-districts of North Bierley, Thornton & Wilsden.*
v.9. *Sub-districts of Idle & Shipley.*
v.10. *Sub-districts of Calverley & Pudsey.*
v.11. *Sub-districts of Cleckheaton & Drighlington.*

Brotton
1891 census index of Brotton (part) Old Saltburn, Easington, Grinkle, Scaling, Staithes, Boulby, Liverton, Moorsholme, Gerrick, Kilton and Skinningrove. 2 fiche. [ ]: Cleveland F.H.S., 1998.

Catterick, *etc.*
1891 census index of Catterick, Moulton, Appleton, Brompton-on-Swale, Ellerton, Colburn, Brough, North Cowton, Uckerby, Tunstall, Bolton-upon-Swale, and Scorton. 1 fiche. [ ]: [Cleveland ... F.H.S.], 1998.

Danby, *etc.*
1891 census index of Danby, Danby End, Commondale, Castleton, Ainthorpe, Westerdale, Little and Great Fryup. 1 fiche. [ ]: [Cleveland F.H.S.], 1997.

Egton, *etc.*
1891 census index of Egton, Egton Bridge, Grosmont, Eskdaleside-cum-Ugglebarnby, Iburndale, Glaisdale, Lealholm Bridge, Sneaton, Sneaton Thorpe and Goathland. 2 fiche. []: [Cleveland F.H.S.,] [199-].

Eston, *etc.*
1891 census index of Eston, Eston Junction, California, Grangetown (part) and South Bank (part). 2 fiche. [ ]: Cleveland F.H.S., 1998.

Guiseley and Hawksworth
1891 census index: Guiseley & Hawksworth. Leeds: Wharfedale Family History Group, 1998.

Horsforth
1891 census index: Horsforth. 2 pts. Leeds: Wharfedale Family History Group, 1998.

Hull
GREAT GRIMSBY FAMILY HISTORY GROUP. *1891 census of Yorkshire: index of surnames for Hull registration district, RG12/3934 to 3945.* 3 fiche. [ ]: [Lincolnshire F.H.S.], 1994.
SIMMERSTER, RON. 'Hull strays', *B.T.* **57**, 1994, 11. Census schedule, 1891, for household of Robert Cunningham of Hull (taken on the night of a party!)

Hutton Rudby, *etc.*
1891 census index of Hutton Rudby, East Rounton, Swainby, Whorlton, Crathorne, Middleton, Ingleby Cross, Ingleby Arncliffe, Potto, Heathwaite and Scugdale. 1 fiche. [ ]: [Cleveland F.H.S.], 1998.

Keighley Area
SPILLER, COLIN G. 'The 1891 census on microfiche', *K.D.F.H.S.J.* Winter 1994, 25-7. List of fiche for Keighley and district.
'Keighley and district strays: 1891 census, Bradford', *K.D.F.H.S.J.* Autumn 1993, 13.

Kirklees Area
'The 1891 census for England and Wales', *H. & D.F.H.S.J.* **5**(3), 1992, 85-8. Includes list of returns for Kirklees area, giving P.R.O. references.

Loftus, *etc.*
1891 census index of Loftus, Wapley and Brotton (part). 2 fiche. [ ]: [Cleveland F.H.S.], 1998.

Marske, *etc.*
1891 census index of Marske, New Marske, Saltburn and Redcar. 2 fiche. [ ]: [Cleveland F.H.S.], 1998.

Masham, *etc.*
1891 census index of Masham, Swinton-with-Warthermaske, Thirn, Ilton-cum-Pott, Burton-upon-Ure, Thornton Watlass, Snape, Well and Rookwith. 1 fiche. [ ]: [Cleveland F.H.S.], 1998.

Mexborough
CHAMBERS, BARRIE, 'Mexborough, 1891 census', *Don. Anc.* **6**(2), 1993, 43-5. List of persons born in Doncaster resident in Mexborough at the time of the census.

Middleham, *etc.*
1891 census index of Middleham, Healey, Fearby, Ellingstring, East and West Witton, Caldbergh, Horsehouse, Carlton, Melmerby, West Scrafton. 1 fiche. [ ]: [Cleveland F.H.S.], 1998.

Middlesbrough Area
1891 census index of Middlesbrough. 7 pts. on 14 fiche. [ ]: [Cleveland F.H.S.], 1998.
1891 census index of Middlesbrough (part), Marton, Acklam, Tollesby, the Workhouse and Nazareth House. 2 fiche. [ ]: Cleveland F.H.S., 1998.

Newton Mulgrave, *etc.*
1891 census index of Lythe, Newton Mulgrave, Ellerby, Mickleby, Ugthorpe, Hutton Mulgrave, Barnby, Goldsborough, Sandsend, Kettleness, Borrowby, Roxby, Hinderwell, Runswick and Staithes (part). 1 fiche [Cleveland F.H.S.], 1998.

Normanby, etc.
1891 census index of Normanby, Grangetown (part) and South Bank (part). 2 fiche. [ ]: [Cleveland F.H.S.], 1998.

North Ormesby, etc.
1891 census index of North Ormesby (part), cargo fleet and shipping in Eston jetty and the dry dock. 2 fiche. [ ]: [Cleveland F.H.S.], 1997.

Ormesby and South Bank
1891 census index of Ormesby and South Bank (part. 2 fiche. [ ]: [Cleveland F.H.S.], 1997.

Pickering
1851 census index H0107 2373 [Pickering]. 2 fiche. [ ]: Cleveland ... F.H.S., [199-?]

Rawdon
1891 census index: Rawdon. Leeds: Wharfedale Family History Group, 1998. Not seen.

Richmond, etc.
1891 census index of Richmond, Gilling, Downholme, Skeeby, Stainton, Marske, Easby, Hipswell, and Middleton Tyas. 2 fiche. [ ]: [Cleveland F.H.S.], 1998.

Sculcoates
GREAT GRIMSBY FAMILY HISTORY GROUP. *1891 Census of Yorkshire: Index of surnames. Sculcoates Registration District RG12/3912 to 3933.* 4 fiche. [ ]: [Lincolnshire F.H.S.], 1994.

Shipley
See Bradford

Skelton etc.
1891 census index of Skelton, New and North Skelton, Lingdale, Boosbeck and Upleatham. 2 fiche. [ ]: [Cleveland F.H.S.], 1998.

South Stockton, etc
1891 census index of South Stockton / Thornaby, Stainton, Ingleby Barwick, Hemlington and Maltby. 5 fiche. [ ]: [Cleveland F.H.S.], 1996.

Stanghow, etc.
1891 census index of Stanghow Charltons, Margrove Park, Coatham, Warrenby, Tod Point, South Gare, Dunsdale Yearby, Kirkleatham, Wilton, Lazenby, New, Old and Low Lackenby. 2 fiche. [ ]: Cleveland F.H.S., 1998.

Stokesley, etc.
1891 census index of Stokesley, Kildale, Ingleby Greenhow, Battersby, Greenhow, Kirby in Cleveland, Broughton (Great and Little), Skutterskelfe, Busby (Great and Little) Seamer, Newby, Easby, Little Ayton and Great Ayton (part). 2 fiche. [ ]: [Cleveland ... F.H.S.], 1998.

Thornton
See Bradford

Whitby Area
1891 census index of Whitby town. 3 fiche. [ ]: [Cleveland Family History Society], 1996.
1891 census index of Whitby villages: (Ruswarp, Aislaby, Newholm-cum-Dunsley, Hawsker-cum-Stainsacre, Robin Hood's Bay, Fylingthorpe, Fylingdales). 2 fiche. [ ]: Cleveland F.H.S., 1996.

Wilsden
See Bradford

5. RETURN OF OWNERS OF LAND.

'Yorkshire', in *Return of owners of land 1873, vol. 1.* House of Commons Parliamentary papers 1874, LXXII, pt. 2, 571-755.

6. DIRECTORIES.

Directories are an invaluable source for locating people in the past. In the nineteenth century, they were the equivalent of the modern phone book, and were widely published. These directories are today a major source for genealogists, since they listed most, if not all, of the substantial inhabitants in the areas covered. Many directories were periodical publications, being regularly updated — in a few cases, annually, but more often every five to ten years. Most of the directories listed here have been physically examined, although every issue has not necessarily been consulted. Many directories have been microfiched; where this is known, it has been noted; however, the fiche have not been seen, so the accuracy of this information cannot be guaranteed. Further information on the availability of microfiche is given in:

RAYMOND, STUART A. *British genealogical microfiche.* Federation of Family History Societies, 1999.

A brief listing of directories held by libraries in the Hull areas is given in:

'Sources for local history, 1: directories in local libraries covering East Riding and Hull, up to 1900', *East Yorkshire Local History Society bulletin* 3, 1971, 3-4.

Many Yorkshire directories cover either the whole county, particular Ridings, or other large regions. These are listed here in order of the dates they commenced publication. A listing of directories for particular towns follows.

The commercial directory for 1814-15, containing the names of the merchants, manufacturers, tradesmen, &c., in Ashton, Barnsley, Blackburn, Bolton, Bradford, Burnley, Bury, Chester, Chorley, Colne, Congleton, Halifax, Huddersfield, Hull, Lancaster, Leeds, Leek, Liverpool, Macclesfield, Manchester, Oldham, Prescot, Preston, Rochdale, Rotherham, Saddleworth, Sheffield, Stockport, Wakefield, Warrington, Wigan and York, together with a list of London and county bankers ... Manchester: Wardle and Bentham, 1814.

BAINES, EDWARD. *Baines's Yorkshire: a new printing of the two volumes of History, directory and gazetteer of the County of York.* 2 vols. New York: Augustus M. Kelley, 1969. Originally published Leeds: Edward Baines, 1823. v.1. West Riding. v.2. East and North Ridings. North Riding portion reprinted on 2 fiche, Melbourne: Nick Vine Hall, [199-].

PARSON, WM., & WHITE, WM. *Directory of the Borough of Leeds, the City of York, and the clothing district of Yorkshire, including Wakefield, Dewsbury, Huddersfield, Halifax, Bradford, Bingley, Keighley, Skipton, Otley, &c., together with upward of 500 manufacturing and other villages and hamlets ...* Leeds: Wm. Parson and Wm. White, 1830.

WHITE, WM. *Directory, guide and annals of Kingston-upon-Hull, Scarborough, Bridlington, Flambro', Filey, Hornsea and the towns and ports connected with the Rivers Humber, Ouse and Trent, including Grimsby, Louth, Barton, Brigg, Gainsborough, Goole, Howden, Selby, Thorne, Snaith, Market-Weighton, Pocklington, Beverley, Caves, Driffield, Hedon, Patrington, and the adjacent towns and villages ...* Sheffield: William White, 1831.

Pigot and Co's national commercial directory ... Durham, Northumberland and Yorkshire ... J. Pigot & Co., 1834. Reprinted Kings Lynn: Michael Winton, 1994.

WHITE, WILLIAM. *History, gazetteer and directory of the West-Riding of Yorkshire, with the City of York and part of Hull ...* 2 vols. Sheffield: William White, 1837. Reprinted on 10 fiche, Melbourne: Nick Vine Hall, [199-].

WHITE, WILLIAM. *History, gazetteer and directory of the East and North Ridings of Yorkshire ...* Sheffield: W. White, 1840.

Pigot and Co's royal national and commercial directory and topography of the counties of York, Leicester & Rutland, Lincoln, Northampton, and Nottingham ... J. Pigot & Co., 1841. Reprinted on 3 fiche, Melbourne: Nick Vine Hall, [199-].

WHITE, WILLIAM. *Directory and topography of the Borough of Leeds and the whole of the clothing district of the West Riding including Bradford, Halifax, Huddersfield, Wakefield, Dewsbury, Heckmondwike, Bingley, Keighley and about six hundred villages and hamlets ...* 15 issues. Sheffield: Robert Leader, 1842-94. Title varies. 1853 issue reprinted as *White's 1853 Leeds and the clothing districts of Yorkshire.* Newton Abbot: David & Charles, 1969. Also reprinted New York: Augustus M. Kelley, 1969, and (on 5 fiche) Melbourne: Gwen Kingsley & Nick Vine Hall, 1992.

WHITE, WILLIAM. *General directory of the town and borough of Sheffield, with Rotherham, Chesterfield, and all the parishes, townships, villages and hamlets within a circuit of twelve miles ...* 41 issues. Sheffield: William White, 1845-1921. Title varies; continued by:

Kelly's (White's) directory of Sheffield and Rotherham, and the surrounding parishes, townships, villages and hamlets. Many issues. Kelly's Directories, 1922-73. Title varies; includes many places in Derbyshire and Nottinghamshire as well as Yorkshire. Various issues have been reprinted on fiche, Melbourne: Nick Vine Hall, [199-].

WHITE, F., & CO. *General directory of Kingston-upon-Hull and the City of York, with directories and historical sketches of Scarbro', Malton, Beverley, Driffield, Bridlington, Hornsea, Patrington, Hedon, Pocklington, Market-Weighton, Caves, Howden, Goole, Selby, Thorne, Barton, Gainsbro', Great Grimsby, and of most of the principal villages and parishes in the East Riding, with the entire of Holderness, &c., &c.* 4 issues. Sheffield: F. White & Co., 1846-59. Title varies.

Slater's (late Pigot & Co.) royal national commercial directory and topography of the counties of Chester, Cumberland, Durham, Lancaster, Northumberland, Westmoreland and York ... Manchester: Isaac Slater, 1848. Yorkshire portion reprinted on 7 fiche, Melbourne: Nick Vine Hall, [199-].

Slater's (late Pigot & Co.) royal national commercial directory and topography of Yorkshire and Lincolnshire, comprising classified lists of the merchants, bankers, professional gentlemen, manufacturers and traders in the above counties, also of the nobility, gentry and clergy ... Manchester: Isaac Slater, 1849.

Collinson Burton & Co.'s West Riding worsted directory ... Bradford: Collinson Burton & Co., 1851.

General directory and topography of Kingston-upon-Hull and the City of York, with Beverley, Bridlington, Driffield, Filey, Scarborough, Whitby, Malton, Market Weighton, Pocklington, Goole, Howden, Selby, Snaith, Thorne, Doncaster, Barrow, Barton, Brocklesby, Ulceby, Great Grimsby, Brigg, Kirton-in-Lindsey, Gainsborough, Louth, Aldborough, Hedon, Hornsea, Patrington, and every parish in Holderness, with many other villages in the East Riding of Yorkshire ... 3 issues. Sheffield: Francis White & Co., 1851-9.

Slater's (late Pigot & Co.'s) royal national commercial directory of the Northern counties. Vol. 1 comprises the counties of Durham, Northumberland and Yorkshire ... Isaac Slater, 1854-5.

Melville & Co.'s directory and gazetteer of the City of York, Kingston-upon-Hull, Beverley, Driffield, &c., &c., containing a descriptive account of each place, followed by a directory. York: F.R. Melville & Co., 1855.

Post Office directory of Yorkshire. Kelly and Co., 1857-1861. 2 issues.

Slater's (late Pigot & Co.) royal national commercial directory of the County of Yorkshire ... Manchester: Isaac Slater, 1864.

Directory of the City of York, the boroughs of Scarborough, Whitby, Thirsk, Northallerton, Richmond, Malton, Stockton-upon-Tees, and Middlesbrough, the towns of Darlington, Pickering, Middleham, Bedale, Stokesley, Helmsley, Kirby Moorside, Easingwold, Redcar, Saltburn-by-the-Sea, Leyburn, Hawes, Masham, Reeth, Yarm and Guisbrough, and many of the principal villages in the North Riding of Yorkshire. 6th ed. Sheffield: William White, 1867.

Mercer and Crocker's general topographical and historical directory and gazetteer for the principal towns and villages in Cumberland, Westmorland, North Riding of York, the County of Durham, and Newcastle, Sunderland ... Newcastle on Tyne: Mercer & Crocker, 1869.

The Post Office directory of the West Riding of Yorkshire, with the City of York. 2 issues. Kelly and Co., 1861-7. Continued as *Kelly's directory of the West Riding of Yorkshire.* 14 issues. Kelly & Co., 1871-1936.

Charlton and Anderson's directory of the woollen districts of Leeds, Huddersfield, Dewsbury and the surrounding villages. Leeds: Charlton and Anderson, 1864.

WHITE, WILLIAM. *Directory of the boroughs of Hull, Grimsby, Beverley, Doncaster and Hedon, the towns of Bridlington, Driffield, Goole, Selby, Gainsborough, Snaith, Howden, Thorne, Patrington, Pocklington, Market Weighton, Hornsea, Hunmanby and Filey, and many of the principal villages in the East Riding of Yorkshire.* 6th ed. Sheffield: William White, 1867.

WHITE, WILLIAM. *Directory of the boroughs of Hull, York, Grimsby, Scarborough, Beverley, Whitby, Middlesbrough, Northallerton, Doncaster, Richmond, Thirsk, Malton and Hedon ... and many of the principal villages in the North and East Ridings of Yorkshire.* 6th ed. Sheffield: William White, 1867.

The Post Office directory of the North and East Ridings of Yorkshire, with the City of York. 2 issues. Kelly & Co., 1872-9. Continued as:

Kelly's directory of the North and East Ridings, Yorkshire, with the City of York. 12 issues. Kelly & Co., 1889-1937. May be an earlier issue.

PORTER, THOMAS, ed. *Porter's topographical and commercial directory of Leeds and neighbourhood, with trade sections for Bradford, Halifax, Huddersfield and Sheffield; also a sketch of the history of Leeds (by John Holmes esq., of Methley), &c., &c.* Leeds: Provincial Directories, 1872-3.

Slater's Royal National commercial directory of Yorkshire. 11 issues? Manchester: Isaac Slater, 1875-91.

The Yorkshire textile directory. Annual. Oldham: J. Worrall, 1883-1950.

Deacon's court guide, gazetteer and county blue book: a fashionable register and general survey of Yorkshire, including topographical and historical sketches, together with separate court guides, and local, postal and statistical information referring specially to Leeds, Harrogate, Scarborough, Whitby and the City of York. 3 issues. C.W. Deacon & Co., 1883-1901.

History, topography and directory of North Yorkshire, comprising its ancient and modern history, a general view of its physical features, its agricultural, mining & manufacturing industries, family history and genealogical descent, myths, legends, biographical sketches &c., &c. Preston: T. Bulmer & Co., 1890.

History, topography and directory of East Yorkshire (with Hull) comprising its ancient and modern history, a general view of its physical features, its agricultural, mining and manufacturing industries, family history and genealogical descent, myths, legends, biographical sketches, &c., &c. ... Preston: T. Bulmer & Co., 1892. Reprinted Howden: Mr. Pye Books, 1985.

JOHNSTON, W., & JOHNSTON, A.K. *The court guide and county blue book of the West Riding of Yorkshire: a fashionable record, professional register and general survey of the Riding.* Charles William Deacon & Co., 1900. Includes extensive listings of the gentry and professions, but not a street directory.

The court guide and county blue book of the North and East Ridings of Yorkshire: a fashionable record, professional register, and general survey of the Ridings. Charles William Deacon & Co., 1901.

Robinson's business directory for Yorkshire ... 1904-1906. Leeds: J. & D. Robinson, 1904.

History, topography and directory of East Yorkshire (with Hull), comprising its ancient and modern history, a general view of its physical features, its agricultural, mining & manufacturing industires, family history and genealogical descent, myths, legends, biographical sketches, &c., &c. Preston: T. Bulmer & Co., 1892. Reprinted on fiche, Melbourne: Nick Vine Hall, [199-].

Mid-Yorkshire directory of manufacturers and merchants and trade annual for 1910. Leeds: West Riding ABC Publishing, 1910.

The Leeds, Bradford, Harrogate, Wakefield and districts trade directory, including Batley, Dewsbury, Halifax, Huddersfield, Ilkley, Keighley, Otley, Pontefract, Ripon, Skipton, &c., 1912-1913. Leeds: J. Crewe & Co., 1912.

Bradford, Leeds, Halifax, Huddersfield and district trades directory. 40th ed. Edinburgh: Town and County Directories, 1938-39. Only issue seen.

Barnsley

The Yorkshire Post year book and street directory of Barnsley ... Doncaster: the Chronicle, 1937.

Beverley

Ward's family almanack. Annual. Beverley: J. Ward, 1836-1920. Title varies. Includes brief trades directory, but not a street directory.

Beverley and district (embracing Cottingham, Hessle, Hornsea, Withernsea, and villages within a radius of about 8 miles from the town) directory ... Derby: W.J. Cook & Co., Beverley: Green & Son, 1899.

Bingley

The Bingley Guardian directory & year book. Bingley: R. Gordon Preston & Co., 1935.

Bradford

Ibbotson's directory of the borough of Bradford ... 2 issues. Bradford: J. Ibbotson, 1845-1850.

Lund's Bradford directory ... Bradford: J. & C. Lund, 1856.

Jones's mercantile directory of Bradford, with Allerton, Baildon, Bingley, Bolton, Cleckheaton, Denholme, Eccleshill, Haworth, Heaton, Idle, Keighley, Low Moor, Shipley & Windhill, Wibsey, Thornton, and Wilsden. Jones & Proud, 1863.

Smith's directory of Bradford and
neighbourhood, including the townships
and villages within five miles of the
Exchange ... Simpkin, Marshall & Co.,
1872.

The Post-Office Bradford directory, 1883 ...
comprising the area of the Bradford
postal district and part of the Shipley
postal district. 16 issues. Bradford: Wm.
Byles, 1879-1928.

Kelly's directory of Bradford and suburbs.
11 issues. Kelly's Directories, 1900-1938.

Bridlington

TAYLOR, WILLIAM. *Taylor's business*
directory of Bridlington, Bridlington
Quay, Hilderthorpe, and the several
parishes, townships or hamlets of
Argham, Auburn, Barmston, Bempton,
Bessingby, Boynton, Buckton, Burton
Agnes, Carnaby, Dringhoe, Upton and
Brough, Easton, Flamborough, Fordon,
Fraisthorpe, Gransmoor, Grindall,
Haisthorpe, Hunmanby, Lissett, North
Burton, Reighton, Rudston, Sewerby-cum-
Marton, Skipsea, Speeton, Thorneholme,
Thwing, Ulrome and Wold Newton,
comprising the area of the Bridlington
Union. Hilderthorpe: W. Taylor, 1888.

Cook's directory of Bridlington, Bridlington
Quay, Hilderthorpe, with the several
parishes and townships comprised in the
Bridlington Union ... 4 issues. Bridlington
Quay: Charles Forster & Co., 1895-1901.
Title varies.

Kelly's directory of Bridlington and
neighbourhood. Kelly's Directories, 1939.

Cottingham

SCOTT, MALCOLM. 'Northgate, 1891',
Cottingham Local History Society
journal **18**, 1997, 5-19. Comparison of
Bulmer's *directory* for 1892 with the 1891
census.

'[Cottingham entry in *Kelly's directory*,
1901],' *Cottingham Local History Society*
journal **17**, 1996, 7-16.

Dewsbury

Smith's directory of Dewsbury & Batley,
with Birstall, Cleckheaton, Gomersal,
Heckmondwike, Liversedge, Mirfield,
Ossett, Thornhill, etc., etc. Bradford: W.
Wright, 1878.

Doncaster

The Gazette commercial and general
Doncaster directory ... Doncaster:
Doncaster Gazette, 1891-1923. Title varies.

The Chronicle Doncaster year book and
street directory: an official guide and
handbook. 7 issues. Doncaster: Chronicle
Co., 1914-38.

Doncaster directory. Kent Services, 1953.

Doncaster directory. 2 issues. Doncaster:
Doncaster Chamber of Commerce, 1957-
1961.

Halifax

COX, J.L. 'Halifax directories', *P.R.H.A.S.*
1914, 271-82. General discussion.

Walker's directory of the parish of Halifax.
Halifax: J.U. Walker, 1845.

Jones's mercantile directory of Halifax,
Huddersfield, and Dewsbury, together
with the surrounding out-townships and
villages, 1863-4. Jones & Proud, 1893.
Reprinted on fiche, Melbourne: Nick Vine
Hall, [199-].

Slater's directory of Halifax and district ...
Manchester: Isaac Slater, 1890.

The Halifax County Borough Directory 1936.
Leeds: R.D. Whipple, Son & Martin, 1936.

Harrogate

PALLISER, P. *Palliser's history and directory*
of Harrogate ... 2nd ed. Harrogate: P.
Palliser, 1840. Only edition seen.

Ackrill's Harrogate directory, containing a
list of residents with their dwellings and
occupations, a list of named houses, and
the districts in which they are situate, a
street guide, with the names of the
residents, a list of the streets, squares,
parades, &c., a list of the hotels, and a list
of the churches & chapels, public
buildings, wells, baths, public officers,
Post Office regulations, &c., &c. 2 issues.
Harrogate: R. Ackrill, 1863-79.

Robinson's Harrogate, Knaresboro', Ripon,
Pateley Bridge & district directory. 37
issues. J. Robinson, 1899-1936. Title and
publisher vary.

Huddersfield

WHOMSLEY, DENNIS. 'A directory of
Huddersfield and district for 1791', *O.W.R.*
3(2), 1983, 28-32. Includes extract from the
Universal British Directory.

Tindall's Huddersfield directory and year book for 1866. Huddersfield: Geo. Tindall, 1866.

Huddersfield directory and year book. 4 issues. Huddersfield: G. Harper, 1867-73. Continued by *Huddersfield & district directory.* 4 issues. Huddersfield: Daily Chronicle Steam Printing Works, 1876-1900. Title varies. 1879 issue reprinted on fiche, Melbourne: Nick Vine Hall, [199-]. Continued as:

Huddersfield directory. 2 issues. Huddersfield: Alfred Jubb & Son, 1909-24.

Slater's directory of Huddersfield and district ... Manchester: Isaac Slater, 1891.

The Huddersfield county borough directory, 1937. Huddersfield: Alfred Jubb & Son, 1937. Includes a 'Who's who'.

Hull

Hull directory 1784. Hull: Hull College Local History Unit, 1996.

Battle's Hull directory for the year 1791 ... to which is added a directory for Beverley. Hull: J. & W. Rawson, 1791. 1st ed. reprinted as *Fac-simile reprint of the first Hull directory, published in 1791 ...* Hull: M.C. Peck and Son, 1885.

BARNARD, ROBERT. *Clayton's Hull directory 1803, arranged by name, occupation & address.* Hull: Hull College Local History Unit, 1996. Index rather than a facsimile.

Battle's Hull directory for the years 1806-7 ... 3rd ed. Hull: R.G. Battle, 1806.

Battle's Hull directory for the year 1810-11 ... 4th ed. Hull: R.G. Battle, 1810.

Battle's Hull and Beverley directory for the year 1814-15 ... 5th ed. Hull: R.G. Battle, 1814.

Battle's Hull directory 1814-15, arranged by address. Hull: Hull College Local History Unit, [1998]. Transcript rather than a facsimile.

Battle's new directory for Kingston-upon-Hull ... 7th ed. Hull: Thomas Topping, 1821.

PARSON, WILLIAM, ed. *The history and directory of the towns and principal villages in the County of Lincoln, including the port of Kingston-upon-Hull and the adjacent towns and villages ...* Leeds: William White & Co., 1826.

Reprinted on 2 fiche, M.M. Publications [199-].

PARSON, WILLIAM. *The directory, guide, and annals of Kingston-upon-Hull, and the parish of Sculcoates, together with the neighbouring towns and villages in Lincolnshire and Yorkshire ...* Leeds: William White & Co., 1826.

CRAGGS, JOHN. *A new triennial directory & guide of Kingston-upon-Hull and the suburbs, with a correct map.* Hull: John Craggs, 1835.

WHITE, WILLIAM. *History and general directory of the town and port of Kingston-upon-Hull and the City of York, with a variety of commercial, statistical and other useful and interesting information.* Sheffield: Robt. Leader for W. White, 1838. Described as 'Part fourth of the history, gazetteer and directory of the West Riding of Yorkshire'. Directories of the two cities only, i.e. not the surrounding country.

The directory of the names, trades, and professions of all persons carrying on business or residing within the Borough of Kingston-upon-Hull. Hull: Joseph Noble, 1838.

PURDON, WILLIAM. *The directory of Kingston-upon-Hull ...* Hull: William Purdon, 1839.

Stephenson's directory of Kingston-upon-Hull and its environs, with a map of the borough. 2 issues. Hull: William Stephenson, 1842-8.

1851. Freebody's directory of Kingston-upon-Hull. Hull: J. Pulleyn, 1851.

Melville & Co.'s directory and gazetteer of the town and borough of Kingston-upon-Hull, Beverley, Market Weighton, Driffield, &c., &c., containing a descriptive account of each place followed by a directory. Hull: F.R. Melville & Co., 1855.

Post Office directory of Hull. 2 issues. Kelly and Co., 1857-61.

Jones's mercantile directory of the shipping ports of Hull, Great Grimsby, & Goole, 1863-4. Jones & Proud, 1863.

Wright's directory of Kingston-upon-Hull and suburbs for 1863. Hull: James Plaxton, 1863.

Mercer and Crocker's general, topographical and historical directory and gazetteer for Lincolnshire, with Hull, &c. ... Hull: Mercer and Crocker, 1870.

Buchanan & Co.'s postal and commercial directory of Kingston-upon-Hull, suburbs & villages, with postal and local information. Leeds: Buchanan & Co., 1872-3. Reprinted on fiche, Melbourne: Nick Vine Hall, [199-].

Butcher and Co's Kingston-upon-Hull directory for 1874-5. Butcher & Co., 1874.

Hull year book and directory, 1876. Hull: William Hunt, 1876. 'First year of issue'.

WHITE, WILLIAM. *White's general and commercial directory of Hull, Beverley, Patrington, Cottingham, Hedon, Hessle, Preston, Sutton, and all the parishes and villages north of the Humber within a radius of 12 miles from Hull; also the towns of Grimsby and Barton-on-Humber, followed by a general trades directory of the whole district.* 3 issues. Sheffield: William White, 1882-95. Designated 7th-9th eds.

Kelly's directory of the port of Hull and neighbourhood. 35 issues. Kelly & Co., 1885-1939. Title varies.

ATKINSON, F., & CO. *Hull and district directory, and Grimsby trades directory.* Hull: A. Brown and Sons, 1888.

Hull and district (embracing Beverley and nearly 150 townships and villages within a radius of about 20 miles from Hull) directory ... 4 issues. Derby: W.J. Cook & Co., 1895-1901.

Hull list of subscribers, including Beverley, Billingsgate, Cottenham and Newland. Hull: National Telephone Company East Yorkshire District, [1896?]

Hull and district trades directory, accompanied with a gazetteer of England, 1928-29. 2 issues. Edinburgh: Town and County Directories, 1928-30. Trades rather than streets.

Ilkley

Robinson's directory for Ilkley, Burley, Otley, Wetherby, Tadcaster, and the Wharfe Valley. 3 issues. Leeds: J. Robinson, 1901-9.

Keighley

'[Extract from Baines' *directory*, 1821, for Keighley]', *K.D.F.H.S.J.* Autumn 1995, 10-11.

'Extracted from Baines directory, for 1823, Keighley section', *K.D.F.H.S.J.* Winter 1997, 26-7.

A. Craven's commercial and general directory of Keighley, Bingley, Skipton and surrounding districts. Keighley: E. Craven, 1884.

Kirkheaton

'Kirkheaton in 1834', *H. & D.F.H.S.J.* 9(4), 1996, 16-19. Extract from *Pigot & Co.'s national commercial directory, 1834.*

Leeds

The Leeds directory for the year 1797, containing an alphabetical list of the corporation, clergy, merchants, professors of the law and physic, manufacturers, traders &c. ... [Wright], 1797.

A directory for the town of Leeds, containing a list of the Corporation and an alphabetical list of the professional gentlemen, merchants, traders, &c., &c., &c., ... Leeds: Binns and Brown, 1800.

A new and complete directory for the town of Leeds, containing a list of the Corporation and an alphabetical list of the gentry, professional gentlemen, merchants, traders, &c., &c., &c., ... Leeds: George Wilson, 1807.

The Leeds directory for 1809 containing an alphabetical list of the merchants, traders and inhabitants in general ... Leeds: M. Robinson & Co., 1809.

Directory, general and commercial of the town and borough of Leeds for 1817 ... Leeds: Edward Baines, 1817.

PARSON, WILLIAM. *General and commercial directory of the Borough of Leeds, including the out-townships of Armley, Beeston, Bramley, Chapeltown, Farnley, Headingley with Burley, Holbeck, Hunslet, Potter-Newton, and Wortley, and several of the principal neighbouring villages, with a list of the streets and public institutions in Leeds.* Leeds: Edward Baines, 1826. Reprinted on 3 fiche, Melbourne: Nick Vine Hall, [199-].

General and commercial directory of the
borough of Leeds, including the out-
townships of Armley, Beeston, Bramley,
Chapeltown, Farnley, Headingley, Burley,
Kirkstall, Holbeck, Hunslet, Potternewton,
Wortley and several of the principal
neighbouring villages ... Leeds: Baines and
Newsome, 1834.

HAIGH, THOMAS. A general and commercial
directory of the Borough of Leeds,
including the out-townships and
neighbouring villages. Leeds: Baines and
Newsome, 1839.

Williams's directory of the borough of
Leeds, giving an entirely new arrangement
of the partners in each firm, with an
alphabetical list, a classification of trades
and professions, and a street directory ...
Leeds: Edward Baines & Sons, 1845.

Charlton & Archdeacon's directory of the
borough and neighbourhood of Leeds,
1849-50. Leeds: Charlton & Archdeacon,
1849.

Slade and Roebuck's directory of the
borough and neighbourhood of Leeds.
Leeds: William Slade, jun., & D.I. Roebuck,
1851.

Jones's mercantile directory of Leeds, with
Armley, Batley, Birstal, Bramley,
Churwell, Farnley, Farsley, Gildersome,
Horsforth, Yeadon and Rawden, Kirkstall,
Morley, Pudsey and Fulneck, and
Stanningley. Simpkin Marshall & Co., 1863.

Johnson's street directory of the borough of
Leeds and neighbourhood, &c. 5 issues.
Leeds: J. Johnson, 1873-1900.

McCorquodale & Co.'s topographical and
commercial directory of Leeds and
neighbourhood, including the townships
and villages within a radius of six miles ...
2 issues. Leeds: McCorquodale & Co., 1876-
8.

The Leeds Post Office directory. Leeds:
McCorquodale & Co., 1882. Not seen.

Kelly's directory of Leeds and
neighbourhood. Many issues. Kelly & Co.,
1886-1947.

Slater's directory of Leeds and district, with
a list of the gentry, &c., an alphabetical
list, a classified trades list and a register
of the principal streets. 2 issues.
Manchester: Isaac Slater, 1890-1892.

Robinson's business directory for the City of
Leeds, 1897. Annual. Leeds: J. Robinson,
1897-1911. From 1898, became Robinson's
Leeds directory.

Kelly's directory of Leeds and Bradford,
1900-1 (with which is amalgamated the
Post Office directory published by
McCorquodale & Co.), with a plan of
Leeds. 4 issues. Kelly's Directories, 1900-8.
Cities only. Also issued as separate
volumes for Leeds and Bradford.

Kelly's directory of Leeds 1900-1. Kelly's
Directories, 1900.

Leeds and district trades directory. 14 issues.
Edinburgh: Town and County Directories,
1900-31. Title varies; Leeds, Bradford and
district trades directory from 1919.

Middlesbrough

The hand-book and directory of
Middlesbrough, Guisbrough, and their
localities. Middlesbrough: Burnett &
Hood, 1871.

Kelly's directory of Middlesbrough ... 2
issues. Kelly & Co., 1885-7.

Mirfield

'Mirfield', H. & D.F.H.S.J. 9(1), 1995, 25-7.
Includes list of residents from Pigot's
directory, 1834.

Morley

'Baines of Yorkshire volume 1: 1822/3 extract',
Cameo 1998, no.3, 22-5. For Morley.

Pocklington

BELLINGHAM, ROGER A. 'Early telephone
subscribers in Pocklington', in CROWTHER,
JAN, & CROWTHER, PETER, eds. Collected
articles from the Bulletin of the East
Yorkshire Local History Society, nos. 1-55,
1970-Feb.1997. [ ]: the Society, 1997, vol.1.
28-30. Originally published in the Bulletin
51, 1994/5, 8-10. Brief discussion.

Redcar

Ward's directory of Redcar and Coatham,
with Dormanstown, Saltburn-by-the-Sea;
Middlesbrough, with the villages Grange
Town, Marton, Port Clarence, and South
Bank; Stockton, with the villages
Billingham, Eaglescliffe, Egglescliffe,
Haverton Hill, and Yarm; and Thornaby. 7
issues. Newcastle-on-Tyne: R. Ward and
Sons, 1926-38.

Richmond

1911: Spencer's Richmond almanac, diary, directory, and Swaledale and Wensleydale book of reference. 2 issues. Richmond: Thos. Spencer, 1911-13.

Cooke's almanack ... and directory of Richmond, Swaledale, &c. Richmond: C.E. Cookes & Son, 1914. '66th year of publication' per cover, but other issues not seen.

Rotherham

Drake's directory of Rotherham, Masbro', Holmes, Kimberworth, Rawmarsh, Parkgate, Greasbro', Brinsworth, Dalton, Catcliffe, Treeton, Whiston, Wickersley, Orgreave, Tinsley, Wath, Swinton, Mexbro', Kilnhurst, Conisbro', Thorpe Hesley, Wentworth, Elsecar, Hoyland, Brampton and the adjoining parishes, townships and villages. Sheffield: E.S. Drake & Co., 1862.

Slater's directory of Rotherham, Masborough and district ... Manchester: I. Slater, 1891.

Saddleworth

BARROW, NEIL. 'The early nineteenth century trade directories for Saddleworth,' *B.S.H.S.* 22(3), 1992, 8-19. Includes list of directories, pre-1850, including Saddleworth, and some facsimiles of directory entries.

Scarborough

B.H. Gillbanks & Co.'s visitors' and residents' directory & gazetteer of Scarborough, Whitby, Bridlington, Quay, Filey, Hunmanby, Flamborough, &c., containing a descriptive account of each place, with a list of clergy, gentry, trades, &c. Hull: William Kirk, 1855.

A directory of Scarborough. Falsgrave 1868, comprising, amongst other information, street directory, trades directory, and alphabetical list of residents, &c., &c. Scarborough: S.W. Theakston, 1868.

A directory of Scarborough and Filey, including the names of the principal householders in the neighbouring villages of Ayton, Brompton, Burniston, Cayton, Cloughton, Garton, Gristhorpe, Hackness, Hunmanby, Hutton-Bushel, Scalby, Seamer, Sherburn, &c., ... Scarborough: John Hagyard, 1892.

Waddington's Scarborough almanac, year book and street directory, 1936. [Scarborough]: [Waddington], 1936.

Sheffield

Sketchley's Sheffield directory, including the manufacturing villages in the neighbourhood. Bristol: [Sketchley], [1774].

A directory of Sheffield, including the manufacturers of the adjacent villages, with the several marks of the cutlers, scissor and filesmiths, edgetool & sickle makers, to which are added the regular setting out and return of the posts and a correct list of the coaches & waggons. Sheffield: Gale & Martin, 1787. Reprinted in facsimile, with introduction by Sidney Oldall Addy. Sheffield: Pawson & Brailsford, 1889.

A directory of Sheffield, including the manufacturers of the adjacent villages, with the several marks of the cutlers, scissor & file-smiths, edgetool & scickle makers. Sheffield: J. Montgomery, 1797.

BROWNELL, W. *Sheffield general directory ...* Sheffield: W. Todd, 1817.

GELL, R. *A new general & commercial directory of Sheffield and its vicinity, in which the names, occupations, &c., are copiously compiled and alphabetically arranged, also, a classification of all that are engaged in the various branches of the Sheffield manufacture ...* [ ]: Albion Press, 1825.

WHITE, WILLIAM. *History and general directory of the Borough of Sheffield, with Rotherham, Chesterfield, and all the villages and hamlets within a circuit of ten miles round the capital of Hallamshire ...* Sheffield: Robert Leader for W. White, 1833.

WHITE, WILLIAM. *History and general directory of Sheffield with Rotherham, Doncaster, Tickhill, Bawtry and Thorne, in the Wapentake of Strafforth and Tickhill, and Barnsley and Penistone in Staincross Wapentake ...* Sheffield: Robt. Leader for Wm. White, 1837. Described as 'part first of the history, gazetteer and directory of the West Riding of Yorkshire.'

Robson's Birmingham and Sheffield directory, street key, and classification of trades, particularizing the residence and profession of the merchants, manufacturers and traders of the following places, Birmingham, Coventry, Dudley, Wolverhampton, and their immediate environs, also of Sheffield ... William Robson & Co., 1839.

RODGERS, HENRY A., & RODGERS, THOMAS. *The Sheffield and Rotherham directory, including Masbro', The Holmes, Attercliffe, Blackburn, Brightside, Darnall, Grimesthorpe, Heeley, Millhouses, Norton, Shire-Green, Tinsley, Walkley, Wincobank, &c., &c.* Sheffield: The Compilers, 1841.

White's general directory of the town and borough of Sheffield, with Esterfield, Rotherham and the surrounding villages & hamlets ... Sheffield: William White, 1841.

Post Office directory of Sheffield, with the neighbouring towns and villages. 2 issues. Kelly and Co., 1854-65.

Melville & Co.'s commercial directory of Sheffield, Rotherham, and the neighbourhood. Sheffield: Thomas S. Algar, 1859.

WHITE, FRANCIS & CO. *General and commercial directory and topography of the Borough of Sheffield, with all the towns, parishes, villages and hamlets within a circuit of twenty miles ...* 2 issues. Sheffield: Francis White and Co., 1861-2.

Business directory of Sheffield, Rotherham, Masbro', and Attercliffe. J.S.C. Morris, 1862.

Hulley's alphabetical and classified directory of Sheffield, Rotherham and neighbourhoods, containing lists of the professions, merchants, factors and manufacturers. Birmingham: John Hulley, 1884.

Slater's directory of Sheffield & Rotherham with their vicinities. Manchester: Isaac Slater, 1887.

The Sheffield city directory, 1895. 3 issues. Sheffield: Pawson & Brailsford, 1895-1900.

Wakefield

SMITH, F. *Smith's directory of Wakefield and neighbourhood, including Ackworth, Altofts, Alverthorpe, Castleford, Criggle, Stone, Crofton, Featherstone, Horbury, Lofthouse, Normanton, Nostell, Ossett, Pontefract, Sandal Magna, Sharlston, Stanley, Thornes, and Whitwood.* Leeds: McCorquodale and Co., 1875.

Slater's directory of Wakefield, Normanton, Ossett and their vicinities ... Manchester: Isaac Slater, 1890.

Whitby

Whitby and district (embracing Robin Hood's Bay and the surrounding parishes and townships) directory ... 2 issues. Whitby: Newton & Son, 1899-1901.

York

City of York directory, alphabetical list, classification of trades, also including the villages of Acomb, Bishopthorpe, Clifton, Dringhouses, Earswick, Fulford, Heslington, Heworth, Murton, Middlethorpe, Nunthorpe and Osbaldwick ... Hull: W.H. Smith, 1843.

Williams & Co.'s directory of the towns and villages within twenty-two miles of the City of York ... Hull: W.H. Smith, 1844.

Post Office directory of the City of York. Kelly and Co., 1861.

Directory of the City of York and neighbourhood. 2 issues. York: Johnson and Tesseyman, 1872-7.

Directory for 1881-1882 of the City of York and neighbouring villages, containing the private and commercial residents (alphabetically arranged), the trades classified, with coloured map of the County of Yorkshire, historical notes, local intelligence, &c. 2 issues. Geo. Stevens, 1881-6.

York and district (embracing Tadcaster and villages within a radius of about 12 miles) directory ... 5 issues. W.J. Cook & Co., 1893-1902.

White's directory of York and neighbourhood. 7th ed. Sheffield: William White, 1895. No other issues seen.

Directory of the City of York ... York: Arthur & Company, 1909.

York and district trades' directory. Town and Country Directories, 1916-17.

York City year book and business directory. 22 issues. York: Yorkshire Gazette, 1920-1951.

Author Index

Family Name Index

Place Name Index

Yorkshire (*continued*)

Goldsbrough 25
Goldthorpe 27
Gomersal 28, 40
Goole 27, 37, 38, 41
Gowdall 27
Grange Town 43
Grangetown 34, 35
Gransmoor 40
Grassington 23
Greasbrough 44
Great Ayton 24, 35
Great Barugh 26
Great Broughton 25, 35
Great Busby 35
Great Edstone 26
Great Fryup 34
Great Houghton 23
Great Langton 25
Great Ouseburn 28
Great Preston 28
Great Timble 23
Greatham 24
Greenhow 35
Greetland 20, 21
Grimesthorpe 45
Grimston 26
Grindall 40
Grinkle 33
Grinton 26
Gristhorpe 44
Grosmont 34
Gueldable 25
Guisbrough 38, 43
Guiseley 28
Gunnerside 26
Gunthwaite 23
Hackness 44
Haisthorpe 40
Haldenby 27
Halifax 14, 20, 21, 28, 36-40
Halikeld Wapentake 16
Hallamshire 44
Halton East 23
Halton Gill 23
Hampole 27
Hampsthwaite 28
Handsworth 32
Hang East Wapentake 16
Hang West Wapentake 16

Harewood 21, 23, 33
Harkerside 26
Harlington 23
Harrogate 19, 28, 39, 40
Hartforth 25
Harthill Hundred, Bainton Division 16
Harthill Wapentake, Holme Beacon
    Division 15
Harthill Wapentake, Hunsley Division 16
Harthill Wapentake, Wilton Division 15
Hartoft 26
Hartshead 22, 28
Harum 26
Hatfield 27
Havercroft 32
Haverton Hill 24, 43
Hawes 26, 38
Hawkesworth 23
Hawkswell 26
Hawkswick 23
Hawksworth 22, 33, 34
Hawnby 26
Haworth 39
Hawsker with Stainsacre 25, 35
Haywood 27
Hazelwood 23
Headingley 28, 42, 43
Healaugh 26
Healey 26, 34
Heath 32
Heathwaite 34
Heaton 18, 39
Hebden Bridge 28
Heck 27
Heckmondwike 22, 28, 37, 40
Hedon 28, 37, 38, 42
Heeley 45
Hellaby 27
Helmsley 26, 29, 38
Hemingfield 23
Hemlington 35
Hemsworth 32
Hensall 27
Heptonstall 18
Hepworth 18
Heslington 45
Hessay 22
Hessle 26, 39, 42
Heworth 45

55

60